LIVING
THE
FIVE SKILLS
OF
TOLERANCE

A USER'S MANUAL FOR TODAY'S WORLD

SCOTT WARRICK

IGNITE
P R E S S
Fresno, CA

Published in the United States by
Ignite Press
5070 N 6th St. #189
Fresno, CA 93710
www.IgnitePress.us

ISBN: 979-8-9850430-0-6 (softcover)
ISBN: 979-8-9850430-1-3 (hardcover)
ISBN: 979-8-9850430-2-0 (ebook)

For bulk purchases and booking, contact:

Scott Warrick
www.scottwarrick.com
scott@scottwarrick.com

Library of Congress Control Number: 2021903666

Cover design by Nenad Cvetkovski
Edited by Reid Maruyama
Interior design by Jetlaunch Layout Services

OTHER BOOKS BY SCOTT WARRICK

Solve Employee Problems Before They Start:
Resolving Conflicts In The Real World

This book is dedicated to the finest, most unselfish human I have ever known, my late little brother, Kelly, who passed away in January 2018 at the young age of 53. His great sense of humor and his constant kindness was a huge inspiration for me as I wrote this book. His humanity towards others was so great that at his funeral, a police officer had to direct traffic due to the multitudes of people who wanted to pay their last respects to this truly great man.

Kelly now watches over everything I do and was certainly helping me find the right words to put into this project to hopefully outline a better way for we humans to live. I would never want to do anything that might disappoint him.

I think he would be proud of this book.

ACKNOWLEDGMENTS

I want to thank my 30-plus "proofers" who proofread this book to help me make it as balanced as possible for everyone.

I also want to thank my cousin, Beth Sheets, for creating the original concept art for the whimsical stick people who look so happy all together on the front cover, with me in the middle of my brothers, sisters, and cousins.

I also want to thank Nenad Cvetkovski, the winner of the international contest to design the front cover of this book. Nenad, who is Serbian, is a single father. My thanks to his talent and his cooperative nature as I constantly made little adjustments to his work.

And finally, but most importantly, I want to thank my wife Lisa and sons Michael and Nicholas who actually had to live with me as I researched, wrote, and obsessed over this book for over a decade. Too many parts were just too overwhelming and disturbing to bear ... and I know I tortured them more than necessary. Thanks again, with my apologies and all my love.

Scott/Dad

TABLE OF CONTENTS

INTRODUCTION

It took me 11 years to complete this book, but it is not the first book I published. I actually made a conscious decision to publish my previous book, *Solve Employee Problems Before They Start: Resolving Conflict in the Real World,* first for a very specific reason. It examines EMOTIONAL INTELLIGENCE (or EI) and EPR in great detail. If you didn't read it, that's okay; we will discuss EPR skills briefly in this book. And for those of you who don't know, EPR stands for Empathic Listening, Parroting, and "Rewards," which is how you should address and resolve conflicts in any situation. Whenever you use your EI and EPR skills together, I call that "Verbal Jeet."

In plain language, my first book examines the most important life skill anyone can ever possess:

> **To Address and Resolve Conflict.**

It is the primary prerequisite for being a leader and building positive relationships. Everything else is secondary.

This book you are reading right now, as well as all the books I have lined up to publish in the future, form a "hub and spoke" design. *Solve Employee Problems Before They Start: Resolving Conflict in the Real World* came first because it is the "hub" of all my books. It lays the foundation for all my future books by taking an in-depth look at developing your emotional intelligence so you can address and resolve conflicts at work and in your personal life, both which require using your EPR skills. Those two skills form the foundation for everything to come.

In fact, you will notice that the first two skills in the Five Skills of Tolerance focus largely on the EI and EPR skills.

In my seminars, I tell the managers, supervisors, and executives point blank, "If you cannot address and resolve conflict, you need to get out of management. You cannot be a leader. Addressing and resolving conflict is the most important skill you will ever need in dealing with people. If you cannot do that, then you need to find something else to do in this organization."

Living The Five Skills of Tolerance builds on my first book. In this book, we are going to look at the five critical skills we all need to master to become more tolerant people. In a world where bullying each other has become so commonplace that between 70% and 85% of employees report that they hate their jobs and are miserable at work, it is time to adopt real, practical changes in how we view and treat each other.

In today's world, we tend to attack each other just for having a different opinion, and it has to stop, regardless of who is committing the attack. It is all wrong.

Think of it this way: If one extremist goes 180 degrees to the right and attacks you, and if another extremist goes 180 degrees to the left and also attacks you, they will meet in the middle and become the same. If you are going to get punched in the face, do you really care if it is from the left or from the right?

What I discuss in this book is not a White thing, a Black thing, a Jewish thing, or a gay thing. It is a human thing.

Therefore, this book is a User's Manual for all humans who want to live in a better world, which must start with one person at a time.

1

OPENING

When I first started conducting my "Skills of Tolerance" program, I remember thinking how much everyone would love it. It went right to the core of who we are as humans and how we can all become better people by addressing these core beliefs:

- We are all human beings, and that means we all share the same curse of human neurology, which includes the fight or flight response.
- No one should be bullied because they are different.
- No one should be stereotyped or labeled with a myth because of their skin color or any other demographic for that matter.
- No one should be denied a job because of their demographics, such as race, gender, ethnicity, religion, disability, height, and so on.
- Racism and bigotry are wrong, no matter who is doing it.
- Diversity, tolerance, and inclusion are issues that affect us all, regardless of our differences.
- Everyone should be able to go to work every day in an environment that is safe.

I mean, everyone will surely agree with these statements, right? Well, let me tell you: I was wrong.

To my amazement, I quickly discovered that there are some people out there who are really offended by what I now call my "controversial statements." Not only did I have some people openly attack me for making some of these comments, but I would sometimes have death threats waiting for me by the time I got back to my office. I quickly saw that teaching this material was dangerous stuff. Unfortunately, what I thought were wonderfully tolerant statements actually lit the flames of hatred in some people.

For example, consider the U.S. Supreme Court's decision in 2020 that gave protected class status to homosexual and transgender employees under Title VII of the 1964 Civil Rights Act. To many people, this decision was very disturbing, much like it was back in 1964 when Congress gave protected class status to everyone regarding their color, national origin, race, religion, and sex. As often happens in the face of such major legal and societal change, the bigots tend to rebel. Will they actually have to work with homosexuals? Will they have to share bathrooms with transgender people? When such changes occur, unfortunately, exercising their bigoted intolerance towards others becomes fair game. Intolerance often increases when someone does not agree with the way society is going. This helps to explain why employment law is now one of the busiest areas of the law in this country.

This should tell you why I now refer to these statements as being "controversial." They all sound good, until we start discussing someone *you* don't approve of or don't want to work beside. These statements become controversial when they apply to "those people."

In other words, we are all very tolerant of people we like.

But what do you think? Were you offended by any of those statements? If not, what do you think of these?

- Not all White people are blatant racists or White supremacists.
- The White guys alive today did not implement the institutionalized systems of bigotry that are in place today.
- Not all White guys support the institutionalized systems of bigotry that exist today.

Do you agree with these statements, or are "all those White guys the same?" If so, you might need to read this book twice, because, unfortunately, you might very well be the biggest bigot in the room.

By the end of this book, I want you to not only agree with all of these controversial statements, but I also want us all to stop focusing on the fact that the person sitting next to you is White, Black, old, young, Democrat or Republican, and so on. Instead, I want us all to start focusing on the one main factor we all share: We Are All Human Beings.

Who Am I? A White Guy Who Teaches Tolerance

I am not someone who you typically expect to see conducting your tolerance program. Actually, I am a White, Anglo-Saxon Protestant straight male who conducts tolerance training.

What is the normal response of people when they learn what I do for a living? I'll give you an example.

Recently, I was flying to California to present this program for one of my clients. Since there are not many direct flights from Columbus, Ohio to Oakland, California, I had to pick up a connecting flight out of Chicago. On my flight into Chicago, I sat next to a young African American woman. We started talking and she told me she was in Columbus for the day on business.

She then asked me where I was going. I told her I was going to Oakland to conduct a training class for my client. She asked me what kind of training I did, so I told her, "I conduct tolerance and diversity training."

She immediately arched an eyebrow and cocked her head to the right as she asked me, "*YOU* conduct diversity training?"

I smiled, looked at her, and said, "Surprise!"

Her response *IS* the norm.

Unfortunately, I get this type of reaction all the time, especially from diversity experts and at diversity conferences. In fact, I am often asked, "What could you know about diversity? You're White." Of course, since I am a White guy, I am also the bad guy.

And yes, such comments are more than just a little bit racist, in case you were wondering.

Please understand, not everyone feels that way. In fact, most people probably don't feel that way at all. However, these racist sentiments are quite prevalent in our world, and since I am heavily involved in the diversity field, I hear them all the time.

For about 40 years now, I have been in human resources, and for the last 25 years I have also been a practicing employment and labor law attorney, where 90% of my practice is related to civil rights. For over 20 years now, I have had my own private practice where I get to tackle the issues that interest me most, many of which are related to teaching my Five Skills of Tolerance program. The skills I teach in the program reflect the way I try to live my life. I consider them part of my religious beliefs.

I did not go into this area of the law by accident. It is my passion. I believe that all human beings deserve basic civil rights. Unfortunately, there are always people out there wanting to take these rights away from others for their own personal satisfaction or personal gain.

Since 1994, I have been a professional presenter on many different topics. So, it was a natural fit for me to start conducting programs on civil rights, diversity, and tolerance. My logic has always been that if we could get employees to treat each other in a civil manner, we could actually prevent many of the legal and harassment or bullying issues that happen all around us.

Actually, since I started teaching these principles within the last two decades, I have come to the following conclusion:

> **Much of what traditional diversity programs teach is wrong...and sometimes illegal.**

Unfortunately, I have seen many aspects of traditional diversity, tolerance, and inclusion programs, which I will simply refer to as D&I programs, fail. If you have paid any attention at all to what is going on in the United States and across the planet in recent years, you have seen that our workplaces and the world need a new way of designing these programs...and we need it now.

"Putting the Cart Before the Horse"

Skill-Based Tolerance
v.
Cultural-Based Tolerance

D&I programs traditionally focus their attention on cultural issues. That means we typically bring people in and train them in some specific culture, which is usually a group of people the organization is dealing with at that time, such as Hispanics, or African Americans, or older folks and younger folks, and so on.

While this is a nice thing to do for those certain groups, it is a huge mistake when you are launching your D&I program. Why? Because there is no possible way anyone could address all the different types of cultures your employees will encounter.

Think of it this way: If an organization trained its employees in sexism, Japanese culture, Chinese culture, and ageism, for example, which would represent quite a bit of training, then what are they supposed to do when they encounter someone from England or someone who is Muslim? Do they simply say: "Oh, wait! I haven't had that class yet!"

Do you see how ridiculous it is to approach D&I this way? In any given week, there are hundreds of different viewpoints we encounter from dozens of different types of people. Are we going to train our people to be conscientious of each nuance of *everyone's* different point of view? Such a task is impossible.

What makes this cultural approach to D&I even more absurd is that within every culture, there are many different points of view. What exactly is Black culture? What do older people think? What are homosexuals like? In reality, there is not one culture on earth where all the people share the same beliefs and values, which makes focusing any D&I program on understanding various cultures even more confusing.

The futility of such an approach should be self-evident, and yet it is pretty much the universal method by which we teach diversity in this country. This is another reason why so many D&I programs simply fail.

Interestingly, in the Equal Employment Opportunity Commission's 2016 report, *The EEOC Select Task Force on the Study of Harassment in the Workplace*, the EEOC said that the way we conduct harassment training in this country is all wrong. In fact, the EEOC says we are really doing more harm than good by the way we teach these topics. I agree.

The EEOC said that our focus needs to be more on building skills so we can create an environment of workplace civility, which means focusing on such topics as trust, tolerance, and conflict resolution.

Again, I agree with the EEOC's conclusions entirely and I have been teaching these principles for over 20 years. We need to start building everyone's skills, just like the EEOC is now promoting. In fact, teaching courses in proper conflict management and emotional intelligence (or self-control) in our schools has reduced the number of fights by 69 percent, bullying by 75 percent, and harassment by 67 percent. This certainly brings more truth to the old Robert Fulghum book, *All I Really Need to Know I Learned in Kindergarten.*[1]

The logic here is simple: If you learn the necessary skills, then you will be able to handle most situations that come your way. It is a lot like learning self-defense. You don't learn self-defense against little people, big people, Asians, White guys, and so on. You learn self-defense. Regardless of whomever you encounter, you will be able to handle the situation.

It is like the old "teach-a-man to fish" strategy. If I give a man a fish (or teach him about a specific culture), then I have fed him for the day. But if I can teach you the Five Skills of Tolerance, then you can feed yourself in perpetuity. You will be able to effectively deal with anyone you encounter.

Over the last couple decades, I have pared these skills down to the ones that I have seen as being the most critical to create that "culture of civility" the EEOC is so desperately trying to institute in this country. These Five Skills of Tolerance are:

1.   Develop Your Emotional Intelligence

2. Overcome Your Subconscious Brain & Resolve Conflict (EPR)
3. Identify & Stop Bullying
4. Understand Real Differences vs. Stereotypes
5. Don't Be an Enabler!

These Five Skills of Tolerance need to be taught to all your employees, as we are going to outline in this book, and then adopted as part of your organization's culture. They should then be your guiding principles. Everyone must learn these skills. They must be coached and then enforced. These five skills should never be seen as a "stand-alone program," which means you teach them and then move onto something else. Instead, these are skills that apply to everything you do, such as your leadership, employee relations, customer service, safety, and so on. These skills should be integrated into everything the organization does where people have to communicate with each other, which is pretty much everything. They should be used to more effectively address and resolve your conflicts with anyone, regardless of the other person's beliefs or demographics.

Unfortunately, that is not the norm. It is rare that you hear someone say, "Oh, yes! We have a strong tolerance and diversity program at work. It trained me to be a better leader, provide better customer service, have a safer work environment, and how to deal with anyone who is different from me. I used these skills to get promoted."

Such a response should be the norm, but it is not. Instead, D&I programs are often viewed as simply being "politically correct" fads or as "necessary evils" in an ever-changing world. They are often not seen as being an integral part of an organization's business model that will help it reach its strategic goals. Rebecca Hastings, the online editor/manager for the Society for Human Resource Management at the time, or SHRM, the world's largest human resource professional association, published an article entitled, *Should Diversity Pay the Price in an Unstable Economy?* After interviewing various diversity leaders and experts, Ms. Hastings made it clear that when the economy takes a downturn, these programs are among the first to go. Why? Because the D&I program was never defined in a way that really tied it to how it could help the organization reach its strategic goals. It is a "nice" thing to do when times are good, but when times are bad, we dump them.

However, you don't see companies dropping their safety, customer service or sales training programs in a tough economy. Why? Because these programs are tied directly to the strategic goals of the organization, so their value is understood. This is just not the case with many D&I programs, though it ought to be.

When the COVID-19 crisis hit the world and the economy plummeted again, those organizations with strong D&I programs that were tied directly to promoting employee engagement and building a safe work environment were able to survive much better than those who had not built such cultures. Whenever employee engagement and morale are high, the ability to be flexible skyrockets. Those companies had a much easier time steering through the pandemic's choppy waters because they could count on their people. They were self-regulating and ready to pitch in. The employees felt safe with their employers, so there was trust.[2]

Unfortunately, that has not been the norm. Most diversity experts are still not making the business case that is needed to tie these programs to the organization's ability to attain its strategic goals. Therefore, these initiatives are still being viewed as "nice, fuzzy, feel good" programs, which is the kiss of death for any program when times get tough.

Successful programs that endure are those that give upper management what they want. This is especially true with a D&I program, which is why the Five Skills of Tolerance fill this role so perfectly. These skills are critical for any organization to reach its strategic goals; they will create the tolerant and civil environment both the EEOC and diversity experts want. It is a win-win.

Of course, once an organization has implemented and adopted the Five Skills of Tolerance as part of its culture, then it would actually be a good idea to focus everyone's attention on the various cultures they will certainly encounter in today's world. Again, it is a lot like learning martial arts. Once you learn the basic moves, you then can spar with various opponents. By learning these skills first, you can then apply them to building relationships and understanding people who are different from you. However, if someone has not studied and mastered these Five Skills of Tolerance, they will never truly be able to resolve issues and build relationships with anyone, or only with people who think like they do.

By the end of this book, you will wonder how any business, as well as yourself personally, can succeed in the 21st century without these Five Skills of Tolerance.

What Is a "Bigot"?

Whenever I teach a seminar on diversity or tolerance, I always define my terms. If I don't, then too many people have their own ideas about what a word means which is usually very different from what I intended to say. Some people are offended over something that I really never said, though it was very real in their minds.

One of the core exercises I do in this program is to have everyone Google the term "bigot." Since the audience provides me with the answer, I have found this to be a very non-offensive way of discussing the topic. It also opens up the session to some great soul-searching discussions.

I do this exercise because the vast majority of people have no idea what the word *actually* means, and most simply do not realize that they have, in fact, been bigots themselves at one time or another. That is just another price we all pay for being human. Many religions of the world actually operate from the basic axiom that we are all born into sin. Boy, did they ever get that one right.

No matter which dictionary you go to, the definition is always just about the same:

- "A bigot is a person who is intolerant of opinions, life-styles, or identities that are different from his or her own." (*Wikipedia*)
- "One who is narrowly or intolerantly devoted to his or her opinions and prejudices." (*Urban Dictionary*)
- "A person who does not like other people who have different beliefs or a different way of life." (*Cambridge Dictionary*)

In the end, all the definitions are pretty much the same:

> **A bigot is someone
> who is intolerant of others.**

It amazes me how often I run into someone who does not mind being called an emotional child. Many people also don't mind being called intolerant. I even hear people brag about being called a bully. However, I have never run into anyone who likes being called a bigot, even though these words all refer to the same thing.

One of the biggest problems with recognizing bigotry is that we always see it in someone else, but never in ourselves. "*I* couldn't be a bigot," we say. "*I'm* a good person."

However, when someone actually discovers the word's real meaning, it is stunning. The vast majority of people are not only surprised to discover what it means, but also shocked to see that it applies to them ... and they probably just did it to the Democrat or Republican sitting in the next cubicle that morning. This exercise forces them to stop focusing on the shortcomings of other people, which is what we all typically do, and it makes everyone take a hard look at themselves. It is one of the most powerful tools I have ever used in class because the audience gives me the answer. It is a fun way to realize that we all have engaged in this terrible behavior at one time or another, so we must all focus on what we need to do individually to put an end to our daily bigotry. Only then will we be able to build better workplaces.

Self-regulation is the key. In order to put an end to bigotry, we need to recognize it in ourselves first. Does this make some people uncomfortable? Of course, it does! But then, that is why we conduct D&I programs. If it was a comfortable subject, then we would not need to address it. In fact, that is my job: To present these uncomfortable topics to my audiences in a non-threatening and fun way so we can all see what we need to do to improve.

In fact, as you will see in this book, the research clearly shows that implicit bias and bigotry proliferates most when it is ignored.

If you do not address these problems, then you are part of the problem. No one ever improves by staying in their comfort zone, and the very nature of all D&I programs should make us uncomfortable. We are facing our own inner demons, and that is terrifying. That is why I never shy away from a subject, but it is important to address this topic in a manner that is as acceptable as possible.

For years, I presented my various programs for a private accounting firm in Indiana where many of the employees were CPAs. I had always had a great relationship with this organization and I presented my various programs for them at their conference every year. This annual conference was their "big show" for the year, with many of their clients and other accounting and CPA firms in attendance. I would conduct a couple of 60-90 minute sessions for them at this conference. My programs would fill an entire afternoon for them.

One year, Alice, a training associate with the organization, asked me to again do a program at their conference that year. The program they wanted was "Living the Skills of Tolerance," which is the subject matter for this book in an earlier iteration. So, I put together the program and sent it over to Alice.

A couple of weeks before I was scheduled to present, I got a call from Alice. She told me that the organization wanted me to cut the bigotry slides from my tolerance program. She told me that they thought the word would be offensive to their members.

"Well, yes," I explained. "That is the idea. That is why it is a core aspect of this training. It is critical to understanding the entire issue of tolerance and getting people to be self-regulating."

"We are doing our due diligence and we think this will be too offensive for some of our members," she explained.

"But I don't understand why you think it is too offensive," I replied. "I have done this program several times and I have never had a bad reaction to it due to the way I present it. You have always trusted my input before."

"Racism is just a very sensitive topic and we would rather steer clear of it," Alice replied.

"But that is the problem. That is not what the word means and that is the whole point. If you look at the definition of the word, which is one of the most critical slides in the program, it is clearly much broader than just racism. Bigotry and intolerance mean the same thing, and this theme runs throughout the entire presentation. They are synonyms and that really drives the critical nature of tolerance home. It is really the key to self-regulation because no one wants to be called a bigot, and self-regulation has to be part of a tolerance program. Otherwise, why bother?"

Now, it is important to understand that this was not a private program for only the organization's employees. That would be a different story. Instead, several of my clients were invited to come to this conference, and many of them were also accounting and CPA firms. So, many of these organizations were familiar with me and my programs.

Also, for the last several years, I charged the firm a fraction of my normal fee to present at their conference because we had a long-term relationship. They helped me when I was first getting started, and I always remembered that. That is what a relationship is, isn't it?

I was also knee-deep in writing this book at the time and I knew what works in these programs and what does not. I did not want to be part of the problem. I wanted my life to be dedicated to doing the right thing and helping others. I did not want to give these companies bad advice or mislead them on a topic as important as this one. Nor did I want to do that to anyone who was maybe hearing me for the first time. There are too many diversity presenters who do more harm than good already. And I did not want to do that.

Granted, there are some aspects of my programs that are not critical, so making edits is really no problem. But this was not one of those issues. Presenting a program on tolerance without talking about bigotry is like presenting a program on the history of the U.S. presidents and not talking about George Washington.

There was a short pause, then Alice replied, "We just think it would be better if this was not in the program. Besides, it is just two slides," she replied.

"Well, in that case," I told her, "I would just rather not do the program. I don't want to give a watered-down version of a tolerance program. I would suggest you get someone else to present a program on tolerance."

"Oh, no!" she responded. "We want you to do the program."

We discussed this issue for an hour. To make sure that we both understood each other, I Parroted, or repeated, everything back to Alice. Yes, it was clear she was understanding everything I was telling her, but she insisted that it was only two slides she was cutting from my PowerPoint, so she did not believe her edits were significant. I adamantly disagreed.

Alice agreed to go back to Betty, the organization's new training manager, someone who I did not know at all, and relay what I had said.

A week or so later, Alice set up a phone meeting. Alice, Betty, and I were all on the call together.

I started by asking Betty why she thought the word "bigotry" would be so offensive to their members, especially considering the exercise I use to present the topic. I told her it is a word that is used all the time in our society and few people know what it really means. It is a critical theme that runs through the entire program, just as you will see it run throughout this entire book.

I then got a vague euphemistic response from Betty, which usually tells me that someone is not telling me the truth. She said, "We just don't think it would be appropriate for our members."

"But I am trying to understand what you mean when you say that it wouldn't be appropriate? This is real world stuff," I explained.

"We just don't think it is necessary and some of our members might be offended. Besides, it is only two slides," she told me in a very stoic tone.

Again, with the "two slides" argument.

So, I quickly explained my reasoning again to Betty, just as I had to Alice.

Betty was not moved. Her mind was made up. I could not use the word "bigot."

After ten minutes or so of trying to understand where Betty was coming from and trying to explain my side, I took a deep breath and agreed to remove the word from the program. Maybe, just maybe, I could be creative and make it all work, but it was not going to be easy. It was not going to have the self-regulating impact the program needed. I told her I would have to rewrite a lot of what I was going to say throughout the program over the weekend, which was no small task, and it all had to be done in three days. So, as long as I was rewriting the program, I asked her if there was anything else she wanted to change.

Betty said, "Yes. We don't want to work with you anymore."

I was shocked. There was a pause because I couldn't believe what I had just heard. After I agreed to gut my program and rewrite it for their conference on Tuesday, she was ending our relationship after all these years.

I then slowed everything down and asked, "Are you telling me because I disagreed with you that our relationship is over?"

She said, "Yes."

Again, I stopped. I could not believe that she actually said that she was firing me because I disagreed with her, which was the very definition of the word bigotry. Nothing could have possibly proved my point better. If you think you are somehow above being a bigot, then you are most likely the biggest bigot on the block.

Since I still couldn't believe the bigotry in what I was hearing, I said, "OK, now, let me get this straight. Because I disagreed with you on this program, our years of working together are now over. Is that right?" I asked.

Again, she gave me a one-word answer, "Yes."

No, there was no misunderstanding here. It was all too surreal.

I have never had any organization tell me that I could not disagree with them, much less tell me that several times in a row, and then be so proud of it, even after I agreed to rewrite the program against my own conscience. Organizations usually want my input on what works and what doesn't, which is why they call me in the first place. They might disagree with me, but they want the most effective program they can get. I also regularly make edits to programs, but never to such crucial aspects of the presentation.

I never presented for this organization again. After about a 10-minute conversation with Betty, my 10-plus year relationship with this firm was over.

Interestingly, I later found out that the decision to remove this word from my program actually came from Frank, Betty's direct supervisor. So, all this time, I was not talking to anyone who could change this decision anyway. It was all too passive aggressive to imagine.

Now, I work with several accounting and CPA firms and I know they would not have reacted this way. However, this was my experience with this one firm, and it was one of the worst examples of bigotry I had ever encountered.

Why could these CPAs not see their own bigotry? Well, they are professional people. They couldn't possibly be bigots, right? They are above all that, right?

Unfortunately, if you think of yourself as being so self-righteous that you are not capable of doing anything wrong, that you cannot make the same mistakes all humans do, chances are you are the worst of the bunch.

If you ever want to effectuate real change, you have to get people to take a hard and realistic view of themselves. Again, since no one wants to be seen as a bigot, this makes people become even more self-reflective. That is the only way to get people to be self-regulating.

Why is self-regulation so important? Because you cannot babysit 10 employees all the time, much less 1,000. We also cannot regulate everyone in the world. To make any program work, you have to inspire your people to want to follow its dictates. That is why you will see me tie all of the synonyms of being an intolerant person together in this book. What are those synonyms? Well, if you are human, like me, you have to work hard at not being a bullying, intolerant, bigoted, emotional child, as I will explain in more detail throughout this book.

Were you offended by any of these terms? I hope so! If not, you may be beyond help.

Of course, if you don't want to become "that" person, then you need to follow the Five Skills of Tolerance. As my wife once told me,

> **"You always think your hair looks good until you look in the mirror."**

Acceptable Forms of Bigotry

Over the last 50 years or so, public awareness of the many different types of discrimination has come to forefront of our consciousness. As a result, our ears have indeed become better tuned to identifying many of the bigoted statements that come out of our mouths. Unfortunately, we still see various forms of acceptable bigotry.

For example, I will often talk to clients on the phone about some issue they are having with a certain employee. Unless the offense is a serious one, I will always discuss how they need to use their EPR skills and coach the person. They need to try and help the person improve first, rather than simply firing them. However, it is very common for me to hear from my client, "Do we really have to do all that? I mean, he's a White guy. Can't we just fire him?"

Oh, yeah, that's why I became a civil rights and employment attorney: To stick it to the White guys. Of course, the person rarely hears the bigotry and racism in what they just said, although I will often point it out to them.

Our ears have become so fine-tuned to recognizing so many other types of racism and bigotry that we simply don't see it when it comes to certain groups of people. Many of us don't hear the bigotry when we make prejudicial comments about older people and younger people, like when we say, "All those young whipper-snappers," or "All those 'boomers.'" We also do this every day with Democrats and Republicans, which is not just another form of acceptable bigotry but encourages all of us to become even *more* bigoted. (Really, not all Democrats and Republicans are the same.) These are all forms of "acceptable bigotry," but they shouldn't be.

So, whenever I hear a form of acceptable bigotry, I will just substitute another protected class in its place so that our better trained ears can pick up on how offensive the discussion has become:

- "Yeah, you're right. Let's just fire the White guy, like we do with the Jews."
- "You're right. These young punks want to take over everything, just like the Muslims."
- "I know what you mean. Those old farts don't want to learn anything new, just like the Catholics."
- "That's right! Those Republicans never shut up, just like a woman."
- "Those Democrats want to give everything away, just like the Blacks."

Did you gasp a bit? I hope so because that means you instantly saw the bigotry in these words. That is what I want us all to do: change the way we think and then shut up before we say it.

Whenever I make these connections for people, their eyes light right up, and I think they want to slap me. Honestly, they really did not see their original statements as being bigoted, but they do once I say that. This is a very direct and fun way of bringing it to their attention.

However, these acceptable forms of bigotry and racism happen all the time. Our culture has now embraced the idea that being White is something we can all mock and ridicule.

For instance, when my youngest son, Nicholas, was playing football in high school, the news was once again filled with more protests and racial tensions. In order to bring the team together and address these divisive racial issues, one of the coaches stood up in front of the entire team and asked them, "Now, who do you think is the 'Whitest' guy on this team?"

Yeah, really.

Even these high school kids, kids whose frontal lobes had not yet fully formed, were shocked at the question. They all looked at each other, understandably confused, and murmured back, "Well, it's probably Warrick."

Everyone in the room immediately looked at Nicholas, who was more than a little concerned over winning the "Whitest Guy On The Team Award."

Later, Nicholas jokingly asked his best friend, Josiah Rawls, who is Black, "Am I really the Whitest guy on the team?"

Josiah, who was trying to make my son feel better about his plight, replied, "That is not even that true."

So, apparently, my White son is indeed White, but he could be Whiter because he is not really "that White."

Clearly, everyone saw that being called a White guy was not a good thing. It was an insult.

Since Nicholas went to a high school that was at least 60% Black, most of the players on the team were African American. Much to my delight, a surge of support came from many of the Black parents. They were outraged because they immediately saw the racism in this question. When they spoke to me about it, I reminded them by saying, "Come on. This happens all the time. Making fun of someone because they are White is a form of acceptable bigotry and racism in this country. It is an insult, but very few people ever seem to care about it too much."

Of course, if I substituted any other type of demographic in there, we would see the bigotry immediately. For instance, what if I asked:

- "Who is the Blackest guy on the team?"
- "Who is the biggest Jew on the team?"
- "Who is the most Hispanic guy on the team?"

But then, every D&I conference I have ever attended over the last 20 years has always had some diversity expert engage in some good old-fashioned acceptable White bashing.

For instance, in 2021, Fox Business News, Newsweek, MSN and several other media outlets reported that LinkedIn Education provided an online training program for its members entitled, *Confronting Racism.* The program was written by *White Fragility* bestselling author and national diversity expert, Robin DiAngelo. Thousands of companies used these programs offered through LinkedIn, including Coca-Cola.

What garnered national media attention was that part of this program urged employees to "try to be less White." The training then gave employees some helpful tips they could use to tone down their Whiteness, such as "be less arrogant, be less certain, be less defensive, be more humble, listen, believe, break with apathy" and "break with white solidarity."

Again, yeah, really.

Of course, in my experience, I have never seen anyone who is Black, Asian, Hispanic and so on ever display such offensive traits. (Insert much sarcasm here.)

The truth of the matter is that Ms. DiAngelo applies these very offensive behaviors to define what it means to be White. In reality, she has given us some very useful traits to help us identify the emotional children of all races. These faults are not just issues for White people to deal with, but they are faults universal to all humans. We all need to work on overcoming them. Suggesting that such immature conduct is the domain of only White people is not just offensive, but it is simply wrong.

Again, as I read this story, I couldn't help but think, "What if we substituted another protected class in there? What would people think then? What if we promoted a program that taught employees to ..."

- "Try to be less Black."
- "Try to be less Muslim."
- "Try to be less female."
- "Try to be less gay."

I hope you also recognize how wrong it is to attribute such offensive behaviors to only one group of people when the truth of the matter is that we all have to strive to overcome our childish conduct. It is the curse of our common neurology.

Even though many people were shocked by this training, I was not all that surprised. I have been to dozens of D&I conferences across this country in the last 20 years, and I hear comments like that, and many worse than that, at every single conference I have ever attended. *This* is what is often being taught by many of our diversity leaders in this country. White male bashing has been a tactic used at every D&I conference I have ever attended.

Recently, I went to an all-day inclusion conference sponsored by a human resource chapter. I like to go to these conferences every so often for a few reasons. First, I am always hoping to learn something new. There are always new ideas and different ways of looking at a topic. Next, I like to see the demographics of the attendees. If you ever want to see who values a certain topic the most, just look at the demographics of the speakers and the attendees at the various conferences across this country. At most of the diversity or tolerance conferences I attend, I am usually one of only a few White guys attending, if not the only White guy presenting. I am always a minority as an attendee. Every time. That should tell you who values this topic, as well as who feels the most excluded.

Interestingly, when I attend diversity conferences where people do not know me, I am often mistaken for being gay or maybe Jewish. I mean, why would a White Anglo-Saxon Protestant straight male ever want to learn about diversity or tolerance, right?

As usual, out of the one hundred or so people there, I was one of the very few straight White males attending. Again, that is the norm.

Yes, this has not changed in 30 years, and it was equally true at this conference. That tells you the same old message is still not getting through to the White males of this country, many of whom are still running most of America's corporations. If you cannot get the vast majority of people on board with your message from all demographics, then where is your diversity?

I also like to see if the same old method of White male bashing will be used again by any of the speakers. Actually, it was worse at this conference than I had imagined. This situation is not getting better. It is getting much worse as racial tensions once again erupt across our country, and whatever happens in the world today will be in our workplaces tomorrow.

At this conference, many of the speakers followed the same format of creating a common enemy that needed to be addressed, and that common enemy was the American White male. In fact, the luncheon speaker showed a cartoon in her program with a group of White male executives and one female executive sitting at a conference table. The man sitting at the head of the table, presumably the one in charge, said: "That is an excellent suggestion, Miss Triggs. Perhaps one of the men here would like to make it."

The room was ecstatic! Most attendees applauded the slide. Several got up and proudly took pictures of it, presumably so they could post this gem of wisdom somewhere on the bulletin board at work. To many people in the room, this cartoon summarized the problems of the day perfectly: White males are the problem.

I saw it differently.

Even though I thought the cartoon was funny, and it did summarize what does happen in corporate America every day, it was still a bigoted cartoon. Yes, many White males do need to change the way they are wired, but so does every other human on the planet. Again, the message here is that all White males are responsible for the institutionalized systems of bigotry in this country and they are all helping to perpetuate it.

I wondered to myself if these attendees would have thought this cartoon was just as relevant and funny if:

- It was a cartoon making fun of a Jewish man ...
- Or what if it was a cartoon making fun of a Black man ...
- Or what if it was a cartoon making fun of a gay man, and so on.

Very few people in the room seemed to catch on to the fact that the theme of the day was to attack the North American White male, like it was a hunting expedition or something.

Now understand, that is not just my opinion. It was the overwhelming consensus of the room. At the last session of the day, the videographer who had been recording these sessions throughout the morning, lunch, and afternoon, raised his hand and stood up. In a clear and commanding voice, he said, "I am a White male, but I am trying to do better."

The room erupted with applause. Yes, he apologized for being White, and he was working hard to be a reformed White guy.

Hallelujah! A reformed sinner has been born again!

Now, here was a guy who listened to these presentations all day long, someone who presumably is not a human resource person but is a technical professional, and the primary message he got from the day-long conference is: White males are the problem in this country and *they* need to improve.

While I admire his desire to improve, this is something we all need to do. In fact, when these "born-again" HR people go back to the ranch and present these great ideas of how White males need to reform themselves because they are the problem, how do you think that is going to go over with the C-suite? This will kill any hope of putting any such programs into their organizations.

They should also get their resumes ready. They will most likely need them.

Again, my approach is quite different: We are ALL human ... and THAT is where I want us all to focus.

The truth of the matter is that you simply cannot categorize "all those people" into one group, and that includes all White males.

This also means that I don't want to be blamed for what my White ancestors did, and yes, they did a lot.

I do not support the perpetuation of institutional systems that discriminate against minorities, or anyone, for that matter. I am an employment attorney and I have often taken cases pro bono to help someone whose civil rights have indeed been violated by a corrupt system. I have fought against those in the system who are perpetuating its evils, which includes powerful people of all races and genders.

However, in the eyes of many people, nothing I do in this life will ever make up for the fact that I am White, just as there are millions of people in this world who will never forgive the fact that others are Black, no matter what they accomplish in this world. It is all wrong.

Interestingly, I have seen that the people who perpetuate these discriminatory institutional systems come in all shapes, sizes, races, ages, religions, and so on. Yes, White males are part of this system, but they have a lot of diverse company. I have personally seen people of every possible demographic abuse their positions of power to bully others.

As time goes on, society just continues to prove my point. *That* is why it is time for a change.

On that note, let me just state right now that we are *NOT* going to focus on anyone's race, religion, age, or gender in this book. Instead, we are going to focus on the human animal. And since we are all human, we all have our work cut out for us in addressing our own racist and bigoted beliefs. We are going to look at how we are all wired. There is no getting around the neurology of the human brain if we are really going to look at human behavior, especially when it comes to tolerance, stereotyping, bullying, and implicit biases. Therefore, I am not going to blame any single group of people. Instead, I am going to focus on the one critical aspect we all share equally: The curse of being human.

Institutionalized v. Individual Racism

In her book, *White Fragility*, Robin DiAngelo adopts the following definition of racism: "Racism is a systematic, societal, institutional, omnipresent and epistemologically embedded phenomenon that pervades every vestige of our reality."

She attributes this definition to filmmaker and scholar Omowale Akintunde.

This is the common definition of racism that I have heard diversity experts deliver for years. Actually, I have lost track of the number of times I have heard diversity experts say that Black people cannot be racists because they are in the minority. The logic here is that no one in the minority can be classified as a racist because they are not in a position of power. According to these experts, you can only be a racist if you enjoy the power of being part of the majority.

However, this definition, which is used in so many diversity and tolerance programs, targets the societal and institutional aspects of an entire civilization. What they are actually referring to is the definition of "institutional racism." (*Dictionary. com*) Clearly, in American institutions, this has been true for many years, and it still happens much of the time today. White people built and have been in control of our institutions for hundreds of years. There is definitely a system of White privilege with our governmental institutions, banking, insurance, employment, and so on, and it is still being perpetuated by many people today, White males included.

It was wrong then and it is wrong now.

However, it is important to understand that institutional racism is quite different from individual racism. So, whenever you are looking at individuals, this is the proper definition you should use to clarify your meaning:

A belief that race is the primary determinant of human traits and capacities and that racial differences produce an inherent superiority of a particular race.

— Merriam-Webster

Yes, anyone, regardless of their demographics, can individually be a racist.

Again, it is always important to define your terms. It is critical that we properly define our terms and specify the difference between institutional and individual racism. Unfortunately, I rarely see this distinction made, which instantly alienates many of the White people in the room, including many of those who were originally on the diversity expert's side.

Punching someone in the face is no way to effectuate real change.

Just as I saw Ms. DiAngelo's training of *Try To Be Less White* as focusing on human faults that apply to all of us and not just to White people, I believe the same can be said for much of her book, *White Fragility*. Throughout my 40 year career, I have had the privilege of working with people from Japan, China, India, Vietnam, Myanmar, and several other countries. I can tell you as a matter of fact, all of these non-White cultures exhibit the same human fault of being very reluctant to confront the issues of racism that Ms. DiAngelo describes in her book. In fact, early in my career, I had to tell a Black foreign contractor that if he brought his slaves to the United States that they would be free as soon as they entered our airspace. He decided to leave them at home. So, Ms. DiAngelo's book is still an excellent read if you think of the title as being *Human Fragility*.

Yes, our American institutions have been built by White men, and yes, there are still many aspects of institutional bigotry and racism thriving within these systems today. And yes, many White men still enforce these institutional systems to the exclusion of minorities, but you can't just lump "all you White people" together, call us all racists as individuals, and say we are all trying to perpetuate these systems. It is bigoted and racist, and it simply is not true.

If you really want to change an institutional system, you cannot go into the discussion by blaming everyone who belongs to a certain group for perpetuating it, even if they happen to be White.

Again, every institutional system in the world is about power, and the people holding that power will often try to abuse it for their own ends. They will do just about anything to hold onto it, regardless of race, religion, and so on. That is because we are all human and we all share a basic set of neurological functions. We will take a painfully close look at our common neurology in the chapter on *SKILL #2: Overcome Your Subconscious Brain & Resolve Conflict (EPR)*.

However, this book is not about addressing the institutional systems that often do perpetuate bigotry and racism. It is also not about the bigoted and racist injustices that have been committed in this country and across the world. Unfortunately, I cannot change these institutions and systems that still exist today. I do not control them. I have no power to correct any of these on-going injustices by myself.

Instead, what we do have control over is ourselves. We have the power to control how we view others and how we treat them. This is where we all need to start if we ever hope to make a better world. THAT is what this book is all about: How we can all become better human beings by the way we treat our fellow human beings on an individual and daily basis. Until most of the people in the world decide to become more tolerant of each other, the institutions of power will not change, because these institutions are run by humans.

However, when the majority demands tolerance, then institutions are forced to change. Apartheid ended in South Africa because the hearts of the world changed, which forced the institutions of power to change. Civil rights improved in the United States because the world saw the brutality of officials like Bull Connor shooting protesters with fire hoses and attacking them with German Shepherds. The institutions of power were forced to change.

The COVID-19 pandemic has proven that the interpersonal power of the individual is one of the greatest change agents on the planet. Its strength is overwhelming because it is based on exponential growth. One person touches another person in some way, who then touches 100 other people, which spreads to millions of people, which spreads to billions. In the end, how we each live our lives matters to others. Of course, whether that change becomes a good thing or a bad thing for the world is up to us. I suggest we all start treating each other in a more tolerant way.

Real lasting change starts in our hearts because we become self-regulating. That is why ...

> **We cannot change the world until we change ourselves.**

Still, whenever I have this discussion with many diversity experts, I often hear the counterargument that many of our American institutions are still based on White privilege. My response is always the same: *Is your goal to change these institutions or is it to start a D&I program for your organization?*

If your goal is to change these institutions, that is great. You might very well be the one to do just that. However, I seriously doubt that is what your CEO wants. Most CEOs want to change the culture of their organizations, which is also a noble role to play in life. That is exactly what I tell employees when I go in to train them in this program: "I am not here to change the world. Instead, I am here to put a 'biosphere' around your organization and change the way you treat each other on a daily basis ... and that is going to be very different from what you see happening in the world today."

However, if you truly want to dedicate your life to changing the world, then you should probably go work for an organization whose goal matches yours, such as the Southern Poverty Law Center, for example. Even then, changing attitudes *must still* precede the changing of our institutions because there is no system in the world that cannot be corrupted by an evil human.

The good CEOs I have met are most interested in building a trusting team environment, and that means adopting the Five Skills of Tolerance into their organizations for all of their people to follow.

That is why this book is for all humans ... not just White guys.

In fact, if every White male on the planet was infected with a new "White guy virus" and we all dropped dead by the end of the week, then some other human would take our place and become the symbol of oppression. That's how the world works.

Our problems are human problems, and we all play a part in perpetuating the bigotry that is destroying our workplaces and our country. The human being is by far the most fickle, most emotional, and most dangerous animal on the planet, bar none. In fact, it is the humans who are currently destroying the planet through deforestation, overfishing, factory farming, and so on, and not the gorillas.

There have been plenty of horrible acts of oppression and genocide committed in this world without any White guys in sight, such as with the Hutus and Tutsis in Rwanda and the Khmer Rouge in Cambodia, to mention a few. This is, of course, not an excuse for any such behavior. Instead, it simply shows that the quest for power comes in all shapes, sizes, and colors. It is a human thing.

Not Assessing Blame and Boomerang Bigotry

As I mentioned before, our approach to D&I for the last 40 years or so has simply not worked. In many ways, it has caused more harm than good by not only focusing on certain cultures, but also by blaming others for the same faults we all possess. This not only kills our ability to relate to one another, but it drives even more wedges between us that later erupt in our workplaces and in our streets. In fact, if you watch any news report, you will see that we are not getting better, but we are becoming more divided, more violent, and more intolerant with each passing year. One side blames the other, so the other side pushes back, and on and on it goes.

We are all human, and humans are neurologically wired not to trust anyone who is different from us. We humans are tribal animals, so anyone who is not part of our group is an outsider, and thousands of years ago, outsiders would kill us.

Whenever you point the finger of shame at others, all you do is alienate the people you are blaming and force them to either resist your efforts or strike back.

It is a lot like hitting an inflatable punching bag that many of us had as kids. The harder you hit it, the harder it comes back. You will never win anyone over if you blame them for all the world's ills.

So, why do White people have a critical stake in eliminating these biases and prejudices from all these institutions? Because ...

> **You will never end bigotry for anyone until you end it for everyone.**

If White people are angered when they feel victimized, then they need to work that much harder to end it for everyone. The reason White people are sometimes harassed or discriminated against is because some White racist once did the exact same thing to a Black person, who then got angry and did it to another White person, who then did it to another Black person and so on and so on.

This phenomenon is called "competitive victimization." Competitive victimization occurs when one group feels that it has been treated unfairly, or illegally, so they feel perfectly justified in striking back at the group, or against some of the individuals of that group, who just wronged them. Of course, once the other side suffers the blow from the other group, they will feel fully justified in hitting back, but this time stronger. Again, it is exactly like hitting that inflatable punching bag. The harder you hit it, the harder it comes back.

> **I call this "boomerang bigotry."**

Whoever victimizes someone one day, that boomerang will come right back at your group the next day. That is why bigotry is a lot like a pandemic. I have to work to save my brother from being victimized today because it will come right back to me or my family tomorrow. It is just good old-fashioned escalation, and it has to stop.

All the policy and legal changes in the world will not make any difference if we do not change the way we think as humans, and that goes double for our subconscious. In fact, the Equal Employment Opportunity Commission said in 2016 that simply adopting policies and procedures without changing behaviors does not do any good. We must all focus on changing ourselves.[3]

Unfortunately, I am human just like everyone else. I also happen to be White. I also happen to be a guy. I also don't want to be a caveman. I don't want to be a bullying, intolerant, bigoted, emotional child. I want to be a good person on this planet. I want to evolve and keep evolving, but that takes real work.

In other words:

> **If you are human,**
> **these materials apply to you.**

A Final Opening Thought:
Black vs. African American

It is important to note that throughout this book, I will be inter-changeably using the terms African American and Black. There are a few reasons for this.

First, I really don't know if someone who is of color is of African descent or not. There are many people of color who do not consider themselves African at all. Some people of color come from Jamaica, the Bahamas, England, and so on. So, I need to be aware of their concerns as well.

I also don't know if someone prefers that I use either the term Black or African American. I really would not know which they prefer until I ask them, and since I cannot ask them in this book, or whenever I am making a presentation, I will switch between using each of these terms every so often. That way, I only offend half of everyone at any given time.

With that, let's forge ahead and try to make a better world for yourself and all the humans you know.

2

THE MACRO CASE FOR THE FIVE SKILLS OF TOLERANCE

E very year, I go to several D&I seminars across the country. At many of these conferences, I am also one of the presenters. As I wait for my turn to present, I will visit other sessions and hear what the speaker has to say. Typical sessions and topics include:

- "GETTING BUY-IN FROM WHITE MALES"
- "UNDERSTANDING THE BUYING POWER OF MINORITIES"
- "SHOWING THE VALUE OF DIVERSITY"

In most of these sessions, I hear the speakers discuss how the attendees must show the value of diversity to their CEOs. They must show upper management how they can increase their business by appealing to more minorities. These speakers also show the attendees how much spending power minorities have in a year, which the attendees are then supposed to take back to their organizations and pass onto their superiors to get them to place a higher value on minorities.

These sessions also try to show organizations the business reasons for increasing the number of minority employees in their workplaces, oftentimes focusing on the negative consequences the organization might suffer if they do not become more inclusive, such as civil rights lawsuits, lowered sales, bad public relations, and so on. Sometimes they focus on showing the attendees why hearing a different perspective from minorities is good for the organization and therefore good for the business, giving the organization a more diverse viewpoint. Such D&I sessions are intended to show organizations how much they need to embrace minorities to survive.

While the concerns I mentioned are all valid points, this approach has not gotten the widespread buy-in from everyone, especially from White males, that these D&I experts had hoped. Year after year, I see diversity people return to their organizations with all this data and new techniques they learned at the conference, but upper management just does not buy it. The ROI (or Return on Investment) from these programs is rarely addressed adequately, nor are the macro or micro reasons for adopting such a program. In short, the diversity person cannot tie the D&I program to the organization's strategic goals, and they fail to get any real committed buy-in. So...

> **No Tie in ... No Buy-in.**

That is why a new approach is needed to tie our D&I programs to the organization's *current* issues and strategic goals. We need to start addressing the issues the organization's executives are dealing with *right now* and stop focusing on the hypothetical issues that might arise in the future.

I never describe the Five Skills of Tolerance as just being the right thing to do, or that they are needed to support the minorities of the company. These are all good causes, but these approaches do not get the support they need from the C-suite.

The Macro Level Need: What Is in It for the Organization?

I recently went into an organization where some truly disruptive employees and supervisors were making everyone's lives miserable. Since all of the problem people were White, no one recognized that the true problem they were dealing with here was a D&I issue.

As I listened to the CEO (a White guy) and the COO (a Middle Eastern guy) describe the situation, I took a few notes and nodded in agreement. As they told me more and more stories about these problem people, I could see their faces growing red and their frustration starting to come out.

After several minutes of listening to them describe their dilemma, I told them what their problem was in very simple terms: "I understand. You are dealing with people who sometimes act like children, but they are still walking around in big people suits."

They smiled at each other and then said, "Yeah, I guess we are. They are acting just like little kids."

"Well," I said. "That is a diversity issue."

They looked confused and the CEO said, "I don't really think we have any diversity issues here. Everyone we are talking about is White."

"I understand," I said. "But you have incredibly intolerant people whose egos are way out of control. As a result, everything is now all about them. If anyone disagrees with them, they throw a little temper tantrum until they get their way. They cannot stand anyone who is different from them or has an idea different from theirs. Has anyone ever talked to you about implementing a tolerance program?"

"Not really," the CEO responded. "I'm not even really sure what that is."

"Well, think of it this way," I explained. "'Diversity' means you have different kinds of people working here with different backgrounds, different opinions, and different ways of looking at things. You clearly have that or you wouldn't have employees ready to kill each other right now. That is a Diversity of Ideas issue. We have to stop thinking of diversity as being only a minority issue. We need to think of diversity as occurring whenever two people disagree or have a different perspective from one another. That happens all the time, like with Democrats and Republicans. Diversity of Ideas occurs whenever you have a conflict or disagreement in your organization. You certainly have that whenever you put people of different races and religions together, but you also have that between management and labor, between older people and younger people, men and women, doctors and nurses, and between Christians and Muslims. The problem arises when we voice our different opinions because very few people take it well when someone tells them that they are wrong. That is why you are having these problems. You have diversity in your workplace every time anyone has a difference of opinion ... and that's when the egos take over. You actually have an intolerant 'How dare anyone disagree with me!' culture here. It is not safe to disagree with each other, which means there is no trust."

"I see ..." the CEO said as he thought about what I was saying. "So, we basically have a Diversity of Ideas going on here and that is what is causing these problems?"

"Exactly," I said.

"But I always thought having different ideas was a good thing," the COO chimed in.

"Yes, they are. Just like having any kind of diversity can be a very good thing, but not if you are trying to do it with intolerant people. If anyone dares to disagree with someone around here, the attacks begin. That is why there is no trust. Every time someone attacks another person because they are different or because they have a different opinion, they are proving that there is no trust. They are proving it is not safe to be different. Diversity without tolerance will kill you, just like it will destroy the personal lives of your people. I am talking about critical life skills that everyone needs, not just business skills."

"But you are always going to have people who disagree and have different perspectives. It is unavoidable," the CEO said in an exacerbated tone.

"Right, and that's why the different viewpoints and ideas we get from our people, which is diversity, will kill any program an organization tries to put into place if we don't have tolerant people. 'Tolerance' simply means that I am not going to persecute you or bully you because you are different, which includes having a different opinion. That is what an intolerant person does, and you can't do anything with intolerant people. That is why so many of your programs are failing now. That is also why your cost of labor is soaring and you are not going to hit most of your strategic goals this year. It is all because you allow this childish behavior to continue. It has to stop. Intolerance is your root cause here, and that must be addressed."

The CEO looked at me and said, "But that doesn't sound at all like a Diversity Program. That sounds more like conflict resolution."

"Yes, and that is what happens when you have diversity and no tolerance. Whenever we have different people working together, they disagree with one another on highly emotional topics. It does not matter at all if the conflict is over race, age, politics, or my job. So, when these highly emotional issues arise, and they pop up every day, you run the risk of having some intolerant employee attacking someone else for their beliefs or their point of view, and that proves to everyone that it is not safe to be different here, so there is no trust. In order to assess the real culture of any organization, there is only one question to ask: Is it safe?"

The CEO looked a little confused, so I continued.

"Emotional intelligence teaches everyone in your organization how they can better control their egos and emotions, which means they are better able to act like big people," I told them.

However, it is important to understand that no one ever gets to the point where they are always in control of their egos and emotions, but we always strive to do better. It is a constant life struggle we humans will always be battling.

"Emotional intelligence and tolerance go hand in hand. Emotional intelligence teaches people to keep their egos and emotions under better control so they can resolve differences like mature individuals. We are then able to be more tolerant, which means we can keep from bullying someone when they disagree with us. Emotional intelligence allows us to be tolerant. This sequence of emotional intelligence and then tolerance applies to differences in race and religion, but it also applies whenever any two people disagree with one another over the cost of parts or scrap. One of the biggest problems here is that we are all human, so we are all trying to use a 5,000-year-old brain that is wired to go into fight or flight whenever someone scares or threatens us. Basically, we are all cavemen and cavewomen in pants, so we have to learn how to evolve and rise above our natural instincts to kill each other."

I then showed them my Diagnostic Diamond for resolving conflict:

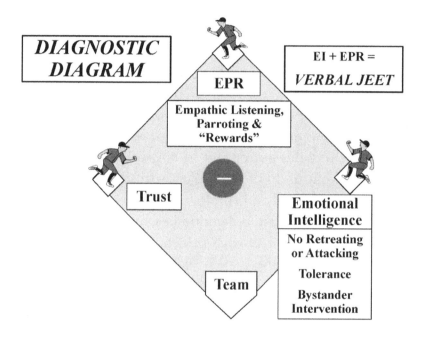

If you look at the diagram, you will see that your first goal is to get to first base, which is emotional intelligence. If you can do that, you can then move onto second base, which is conflict resolution. This is where I use my EPR skills, which stands for Empathic Listening, Parroting and "Rewards." (I will discuss these EPR skills later in this book in more detail. Also, I always put the word "Rewards" in quotations because we are not talking about a physical reward, such as money. Rather, we are talking about a psychological reward, which, to a human, is worth much more.) Then, if you can make it to second base, getting to third base is easy. If you can show that other person that it is safe to disagree with you, that builds trust. That is our ultimate goal: Creating a SAFE workplace. That is trust.

"I see," the CEO considered out loud.

"But this sounds more like an employee relations strategy, not a diversity program," the COO chimed in.

"I know, and isn't that sad? Diversity occurs all around us every minute of every day. Emotional intelligence and tolerance teach us how to control ourselves better and not bully other people because they are different, which always happens whenever we disagree with each other. If you just follow this diagram, not only can you diagnose why any conflict that comes your way has gotten out of control, but you will also see exactly what to do to build trust with the people around you. It is the best legal and employee relations strategy I know. Workplace violence issues, legal issues, and morale issues all come from one source: A toxic work environment, which means it is not safe," I explained.

I then handed them each a copy of my book, *Solve Employee Problems Before They Start: Resolving Conflict In The Real World*, and told them they needed to read it ... all of it. Yes, I saved them a trip to Amazon.

I then added, "That is why your relationship with the union is so bad. If managers and supervisors were acting like big people and weren't bullying the employees, then the union leadership and its members wouldn't be retaliating against you all the time. That is why your scrap rate is so high, as are your grievances."

"Yes! Did you see the scrap rate for last month? I know we had this ridiculous scrap rate because employees were trying to stick it to us," the CEO shot back as the sweat beaded up on his forehead.

"That is probably true," I said. "But is that going to really be your response: They started it? We have to resolve these conflicts, not escalate them. Again, that requires tolerance. I have seen your supervisors and managers at work, and I can tell you, that is exactly why you have a union in the first place. It is not safe to disagree with your supervisors and managers. So, there is no trust at all on your shop floor. If these shop employees disagree with your supervisors, your management team will get them. That is really the only question you will ever need to ask in evaluating your culture: Is it safe to disagree with someone here, especially with someone who is a supervisor or a manager? And the answer to that question on your shop floor is clear: No, it is not."

I then typically explain that my Five Skills of Tolerance are what they need to solve these problems. The first two skills are the most critical, which are emotional intelligence and then learning how to control and overcome your subconscious or implicit biases so you can resolve conflict with your EPR skills. These first two skills are the most critical life skills anyone can master in today's world. Once we have addressed those two skills, we want to make sure your people can spot bullying when it happens, and then stop it. That is the third skill. The fourth skill teaches them how to distinguish between the real differences that exist between us and all of the stereotypes and myths they have always heard about other people. And finally, the fifth skill requires everyone in the workplace to take responsibility for speaking up and stop enabling others who break these rules. Those are the Five Skills of Tolerance every workplace, as well as the world, needs.

After that, they were sold. I never ever try to convince my clients to adopt a new D&I program because having more minorities will help their business or anything like that. I discover what issues THEY are *already* dealing with and show them how the Five Skills of Tolerance program can help solve the Diversity of Ideas problems that *already exist within their organization*. There is one approach for everything because everyone is always dealing with the human animal. If you are dealing with humans, this is the program you need.

Of course, once an organization has established a culture that demands the Five Skills of Tolerance, hiring and promoting people based upon their skills, regardless of race, religion, or any other demographic, dominates the culture. Once we have better control over our egos and emotions, as well as our implicit biases, then issues like race, religion, and politics are all much easier to address and resolve. Your employees will be better prepared to see someone else's point of view. They won't feel so threatened by someone who is different, which is killing our society and making it difficult to engage each other in a productive dialogue.

I always approach this issue of the Diversity of Ideas by teaching the Five Skills of Tolerance ... *NOT* by addressing each individual culture, which does not work. It never has and it never will.

Unfortunately, approaching D&I issues in this manner is a rarity. But then, that is why you are reading this book, isn't it?

3

THE MICRO CASE FOR THE FIVE SKILLS OF TOLERANCE

Even if the executives buy into this program at the macro-level, that does not mean that the Five Skills of Tolerance program will be supported by the employees. Of course, few people today will stand up and say, "I am against diversity and tolerance. I have better things to do." Most people do not want to look like a bigot. Instead, people just simply won't support it. So, passive resistance ends up killing the program because most people find more important things to do rather than come to a D&I event. It simply dies on the vine.

Enthusiastic buy-in is needed for any program to not only survive, but to thrive. You must have enthusiastic support for the Five Skills of Tolerance if it is to ever become self-regulating.

The United States Supreme Court and the *Ricci* Case

In *Ricci, et al. v. DeStefano*, the United States Supreme Court heard a case that brought the worst fears many people have over the issue of diversity in the workplace to the forefront of this debate in America. This case directly addressed the greatest micro issue most of us face: **JOBS**

(For a more detailed account of this case, just go to my website at www.scottwarrick.com and look under the *Living The Five Skills of Tolerance* icon.)

In *Ricci*, the New Haven Fire Department had eight positions open for lieutenant and seven positions available for captain. In keeping with its standard process, any firefighter who wanted to be considered for these positions was required to take an examination for that job.

Since the White firefighters scored the highest on the lieutenant's exam, all the lieutenant positions were filled by Whites. As for the captain's exam, a Hispanic firefighter and White firefighters received the highest scores. None of the Black firefighters scored high enough to be promoted.

So, in January 2004, Thomas Ude, New Haven City's Legal Counsel, had a meeting with Industrial/Organizational Solutions, Inc. (or IOS) Vice President Chad Legel, who was the leader of the IOS team that developed and administered these tests. Based solely on the statistical results of the test, the New Haven City officials claimed that the examinations had illegally discriminated against minority candidates. However, in this meeting, Legel defended the validity of both examinations.

In designing these exams, IOS representatives interviewed incumbent captains and lieutenants and their supervisors to determine the essential tasks, knowledge, skills, and abilities that were essential for the lieutenant and captain positions. They rode along with and observed other on-duty firefighters. At every stage of the job analyses, IOS deliberately oversampled minority firefighters to ensure that the results, which IOS would use to develop the examinations, would not unintentionally favor White candidates.

After IOS prepared the tests, the city opened a three-month study period. IOS then gave the firefighters a list that showed them where they could find all the answers to the examination's questions in the study materials they were given. Therefore, all the material for the examinations was taken directly from approved source materials, which were all derived directly from duties required to successfully perform these positions. In other words, IOS designed these tests to be as unbiased and as legally defensible as possible.

In order to understand this area of the law, it is important to understand the two primary theories of illegal discrimination that exist under Title VII of the 1964 Civil Rights Act:

> **Disparate treatment and
> disparate impact**

Under disparate treatment, or bad treatment, the theory is that an employer *intentionally* discriminated against an employee or prospective employee based upon his/her protected class status, such as race, color, sex or age, to mention a few. This is what most people think of when it comes to illegal discrimination.

However, under a theory of disparate impact, or bad impact, the employer did *not intend* to discriminate against anyone. Instead, an employer has adopted a policy or practice that unintentionally discriminates against a group of protected class individuals.

In order to establish a prima facie (or first sight) case of disparate impact, the Black firefighters had to show that there was a significant statistical difference between how many Black firefighters passed the test and the number of Hispanic and

White firefighters who passed the test. In this case, there was in fact a significant statistical difference between the two groups.

In order to defend itself, New Haven then needed to show that these tests were job-related for the position in question and consistent with business necessity. If New Haven could show that these tests were job-related, then the Black firefighters would have to show that the city had another alternative employment practice available that had less of a disparate impact and that the city failed to use it.

Of course, thanks to all the precautions IOS had taken to ensure these tests were free of bias, no such arguments existed.

In order for the firefighters who passed with the highest scores to receive their promotions, the New Haven Civil Service Board (or the CSB) had to approve the results of these tests. Instead, the city claimed that these test results presented a case of disparate impact and therefore illegally discriminated against the Black firefighters.

Of course, as you now know, the city's attorney clearly misstated the law.

Now, wouldn't that make you pause and wonder why Ude would make such a mistake? How could he misinterpret the law on this issue so badly? Does it make you wonder if an alternative agenda is at work here? Read on, because the truth will come out later.

Ronald Mackey, a representative from the International Association of Black Professional Firefighters, argued that a validation study was necessary. However, he also suggested that the city give additional points to the Black firefighters who took the test so more of them could be promoted into these positions over some of the Hispanic and White firefighters.

However, this practice, which is called "norming" test scores, became illegal in 1991. So, when Mackey made this suggestion, it had already been illegal for over a decade.

At the next meeting, on March 11, 2004, the CSB heard from several witnesses regarding the validity of these tests.

One of the witnesses the CSB spoke to was Vincent Lewis, a Black fire program specialist for the Department of Homeland Security and a retired fire captain from Michigan. Lewis concluded that the "questions were relevant for both exams." Actually, Lewis claimed that the New Haven candidates had an advantage because the study materials identified exactly where the firefighters could find the answers to the questions on the upcoming exams. Lewis said that in other fire departments, by contrast, "you had to know basically the . . . entire book."

Lewis concluded that any disparate impact that might have occurred was most likely due to the fact that Whites usually "outperform some of the minorities on testing" because "more Whites . . . take the exam." In other words, Lewis said that the statistical calculations were unreliable because the raw numbers were too small to be statistically significant.

For example, let's say 80 Whites take a standardized test and 14 Blacks take the same test. (I chose these numbers because these are approximately the percentages of Whites and Blacks making up the total population of the United States according to the 2000 census, which is the census most applicable to this time period.) Let's then say that 40 Whites (or 50%) pass the test and 4 Blacks (or 29%) pass the test. These failure rates of the White and Black employees would present an inference of disparate impact under the law.

However, when you look at the raw numbers themselves, 40 Whites failed while only 10 Blacks failed. In other words, **four times** as many Whites failed the test as Blacks.

Does this mean that Whites are not as smart as Blacks?

Does that mean that there is a racial prejudice against Whites? Not at all.

The issue Lewis was bringing to the CSB's attention is clear. He said: "You cannot consider the statistical analysis in a vacuum. At some point, the raw numbers become so disproportionate to one another that the statistical comparison between the two groups becomes meaningless. The raw data itself must be statistically significant."

This would be the same thing if I walked up to ten children in New York and asked them where the Statue of Liberty is located. If five get it right and five get it wrong, I could come to the erroneous conclusion that half of the kids in New York do not know where the Statue of Liberty is located. So, I conclude that half of the kids in New York City are not very smart.

Of course, that is an inaccurate conclusion because asking only ten children is not a representative sample of the number of children living in New York City. However, that is basically what Lewis is saying happens when you compare the pass/fail rates between Whites and Blacks if the raw numbers do not represent a statistically significant number of applicants.

In fact, all of the experts who addressed the city on this issue agreed with Lewis.

Still, the city refused to certify the examination results, which resulted in this lawsuit.

On June 29, 2009, the U.S. Supreme Court delivered its opinion in the *Ricci* case. In a 5 to 4 decision, the Court held for Ricci and his fellow White and Hispanic firefighters.

Of course, once the city found itself in front of the U.S. Supreme Court, the truth of this case came out:

The city chose to not certify the results of the tests **because it was afraid that it would be sued by the Black firefighters** under a theory of disparate impact.

Therefore, the city's position was that ...

It should be allowed to discriminate against the Hispanic and White firefighters who scored the highest on the examinations in order to avoid getting sued by the Black firefighters.

Yes, the city actually chose to illegally discriminate against the Hispanic and White firefighters in order to avoid getting sued by the Black firefighters.

So, do you still agree with the controversial statements I made at the beginning of this book?

- No one should ever be denied a job or a promotion because of their demographics, such as race, color, religion, sexual orientation.
- Racism and bigotry are wrong, no matter who is doing it.

The U. S. Supreme Court agreed with these statements.

The Court held that the city illegally discriminated against the Hispanic and White firefighters because it decided not to certify the results of the exams based on their race. The Court said that there was no evidence that these tests were flawed in any way. There was also no evidence presented by the city that showed there were other equally valid and less discriminatory methods available.

The Rise of Racism in America

Again, you cannot end the institutional systematic discrimination against any single group of people by penalizing or discriminating against another group of people. This is the problem our society has been facing since illegal quota systems became the subject of numerous legal proceedings. Discriminating against one group will only foster the seeds of retaliation, which leads us right back to competitive victimization, or what I like to refer to as boomerang bigotry.

It must stop. Everyone loses.

That is why ...

> **You will never end bigotry for anyone until you end it for everyone.**

The *Ricci* case represented some of greatest fears of many different people, Whites, Hispanics, Asians, and Blacks alike, such as:

> If I am not Black, will I be discriminated against when I try to get a job, a promotion, and so on? Is this going to happen to my kids in the future? Do qualifications matter, or do the statistics count more, regardless of whether they are reliable or not?
>
> If I am Black, will I be given a fair shot because of my skin color? If I am Black and earn my position, will people say I got it only because of my race? Is this only adding to the myth that Black people do not want equal treatment but better treatment? Does this add to the myth that Black people are not as smart as Whites so they cannot compete with them intellectually?

On the other hand, such illegal discrimination against the Hispanic and White firefighters gives White supremacists all the fodder they need to say:

- "See, I told you Blacks are not as smart as Whites."
- "See, I told you Blacks are lazy and won't study when they need to."

- "See, I told you Blacks have an entitlement mentality and want everything handed to them."

I know the truth does not lie in any of these myths, but many people who already harbor these prejudices see this case as proof that every negative myth or stereotype they have always thought about minorities is true.

My White Guy Story

When I graduated from high school, I had a lot of potential, but no money. So, to get my undergraduate degree, I went to work at Owens Corning Fiberglas and made glass wool, which tastes terrible, by the way. The factory would get so hot that my pores would open and the micro-shards of glass wool would get into my pores, eyes, ears, and mouth. However, it paid for most of my undergraduate degree at The Ohio State University. Along with getting as many student loans as I could, working three jobs at a time and every so often selling my plasma, I was able to afford college.

I lived at home for two years and went to the OSU branch in Newark, Ohio where I got a great education. I then moved to the main campus in my junior year, which cost substantially more in tuition. I also had to pay for room and board. So, I took on various jobs, sold more of my plasma, which included a complimentary donut, and I went to class and studied whenever I could. Actually, my undergraduate degree had the lowest GPA of any of my college degrees, largely because it is hard to do well on a test when you do not have time to study.

When I graduated from Ohio State, I wanted to go to law school. However, again, there was no money. So, I worked for two years, sold vacuum cleaners door to door, worked at Wendy's and then worked in an aluminum factory as a United

Steelworker, where I sustained a skull fracture because someone named "Pothead Larry" did not secure a coil of aluminum properly on the previous shift. Yes, I am a big believer in substance abuse testing these days.

I saved all the money I could and even paid my parents rent. I was no longer living anywhere for free.

I was then accepted into the Master of Labor and Human Resources program at The Ohio State University. It was a six-quarter program, but I only had enough money for four quarters. So, I crammed as many courses into each quarter as the university would let me. I then finished within my four-quarter time frame with exactly $107.00 left to my name.

I worked in human resources for the next few years, got married in 1987, and then enrolled in the evening program at Capital University College of Law in the fall of 1992. Four years of working at a bank in human resources during the day and going to law school at night laid ahead of me. Since taking pills to stay awake seemed too druggy for me, I drank Mt. Dew. So, across the next few years of law school, I destroyed my stomach lining. (Maybe I should have taken the pills, like Elvis did.)

I tell you this story because I am just like many people. There is really nothing all that special about how I got my education. Nothing was ever given to me so I could get through college, which is true for most of us.

Today, with almost 40 years of human resources and 25 years of employment law experience behind me, I have seen many instances where White privilege did indeed kick in and get a White person the job over someone who was Black and equally as qualified. It was wrong then and it is still wrong today.

Interestingly, however, the opposite happens to me all the time.

Since my career has been largely focused in the HR field, I have been told point blank that even though my potential employers loved my background and my work, they "really needed an African American" or they "really needed a woman" running their HR department. Yes, this has happened more than once throughout my career, probably more than most people, which shouldn't be too surprising since human resources is a field that is largely dominated by women. Also, the HR profession across the last 40 years has probably focused more on the inclusion of minorities than others. Actually, the main reason I went back to law school was so I would be more qualified than the Black and female candidates I was competing against, as well as the Baby Boomers, who were always just a few years ahead of me … and there were a lot of them.

Even when it comes to presenting seminars on my Five Skills of Tolerance, I am often told, "We really need someone Black to conduct our diversity training," even though these HR people had seen my program and wanted it for their organizations. It made no difference how good my program was or how good I was at presenting it, I was the wrong color. Interestingly, this illegal racial discrimination still happens to me quite often.

A few years ago, I got a call from a large Ohio government agency. I was asked if I would be interested in presenting my full day leadership session for their management team. Some employees at the agency heard me present and they wanted me to come in and conduct a program for their people. I agreed and then designed a full day program for the organization. After I sent it over for their review, we chose a date for the training. They were inked into my calendar. We were all set … or so I thought.

I later got a call from the agency telling me that it had decided to mark this project as an MBE program.

MBE? I had never heard of that before, so I asked the person what this meant.

She explained that an MBE is the Minority Business Enterprise program where only minority-owned businesses could bid on a project. Actually, 15% of all the state's contracts are designated as MBE programs.

"But I have already written the program. I have already submitted it to the people who called me," I explained.

"Well," the woman said, "unless you are a minority-owned business, you will not be eligible to submit a bid for this program."

"But your people called me," I explained. "There was no bidding involved. Actually, I don't submit bids to state government agencies because they typically go with the Wal-Mart pricing."

"I'm sorry, but in order to be fair, we have designated this project as an MBE," she replied.

"Fair? How is this fair?" I asked.

"Well, minority-owned businesses need to be given a chance to get government contracts. So, this is a fair system to help them get these contracts," she explained.

"How is this fair?" I asked. "I am a sole proprietor. It is just me. I compete against other employment attorneys, human resource professionals, and trainers the same as anyone else. If you designate 15% of all the contracts given out by the state of Ohio as only going to minorities, then I am not allowed to compete at all because I am White. It is Jackie Robinson in reverse. This is not only unfair, it is clearly illegal," I argued.

"No, it is not," the person replied.

"Oh, yes, it is," I shot back.

In 2003, the University of Michigan gave an additional 20 points out of a 100-point total to certain minorities to gain admission into the University over Whites.

In *Gratz v. Bollinger*, 539 U.S. 244, the United States Supreme Court ruled that the University was using an illegal quota system that violated the Equal Protection Clause of the Constitution, or the 14th Amendment. The Court held that giving minority applicants an additional 20 points made race *THE* decisive factor for admission and not *A* factor to consider. That means it illegally discriminated against White people.

Now, the state of Ohio can make race *a* factor in a small percentage of contracts, but 15% is a quota system. It is illegal. The problem is that no one has spent the vast amount of money to challenge Ohio's MBE system in front of the U.S. Supreme Court under the *Gratz* decision.

In *Grutter v. Bollinger*, the Court said, "We expect that 25 years from now, the use of racial preferences will no longer be necessary," which was prophetic. According to the U.S. Census, almost three times as many White people live in poverty as do Black people and almost six times more Whites fell into poverty from 2019 to 2020 than did Blacks. Discriminating against *anyone* will only result in more boomerang bigotry.

There was a long pause on the other end.

The woman then spoke up and said, "I am sure we can get someone just as good as you. This is what we need to do to be fair."

She then hung up on me.

All of a sudden, the *Ricci* case popped back into my head. This time, however, the United States Supreme Court was not there to help me.

I included this experience in this book because it happens every day to several business owners who are not minorities. Again, discrimination is wrong whenever it happens to anyone. It will all end in boomerang bigotry.

According to the U.S. Census, millions more White people fell below the poverty line from 2019 to 2020 for the first time than Black people. In fact, almost three times as many White people live in poverty than do Black people. Quite frankly, I don't think any child should go hungry, regardless of their race. No one should be discriminated against, and for that, I am labeled a bigot and a racist. It is all wrong.

What is even more disturbing is that I have several clients who do qualify to bid on state MBE contracts because they hired a minority partner into their organization just so they could get some of these contracts. In other words, they are scamming the MBE system. In these specific cases, the minority partner is a stakeholder, so that person gets paid a bonus every time the company is awarded an MBE contract. The organization then simply increases their bid to cover the additional cost. In the end, the taxpayers pay more for the same services.

Interestingly, no one has ever told me they need someone taller.

Many of our more liberal leaders and civil rights organizations have also come out and declared this type of illegal discrimination just plain wrong.

Kamala Harris, Vice President of the United States, said: "Let me be clear: equal rights are not extra rights."[4]

Additionally, GLAAD, or the Gay & Lesbian Alliance Against Defamation, says right on its website that lesbian, gay, bisexual, and transgender people want equal rights, not special rights.[5]

Again, let me make this perfectly clear:

> **You cannot discriminate against individuals to solve a systematic institutional problem.**

Diversity and You

Do some diversity experts profess and teach human resource people how to illegally discriminate against White people to boost the employment numbers of minorities?

Yes, I am afraid so. I have heard it many times myself.

At one national human resource conference, I decided to go to a diversity session entitled, "Measuring Inclusion in Your Organization." I thought that sounded like an interesting title, so I grabbed a seat near the front and listened to the speaker, who was presumably an expert diversity consultant. I was sitting between two HR people I knew from a large Ohio employer. One was a White female and one was a Black male.

As the speaker continued, he said we needed to hold managers and directors accountable for their diversity numbers. Goals had to be set and if these managers did not meet their goals, they needed to be penalized.

This all sounded good, I thought. If you interview enough qualified people of different demographics, and if you have mastered your subconscious biases, then the numbers should be fair in the end. Fairly hiring people is a lot like reaching into a jar where there are 50 white marbles, 30 black marbles, and 20 brown marbles all equally dispersed throughout the jar. If you grab a big handful of marbles and pull them out of the jar, then you should get a representative sample. Being in HR for over four decades, I can attest this is true. So, I liked what I was hearing.

The speaker went on to explain that if a manager's goal requires him to have a certain number of minorities working for him by the end of the year, but he fails to meet this goal, then the manager's pay should be cut ... sometimes by as much as $20,000 per year.

Now THAT got my attention. My head popped up to attention, as did my two HR friends from Ohio, who were also well versed in employment law. I was shocked. I wasn't sure if I actually heard him correctly. Was he really saying that he was setting quotas for his clients, which has been illegal for years? Was he also saying if I was a manager who did not hire a certain number of minorities that my pay would be cut?

At that point, someone asked that very question. The speaker confirmed that was in fact what he was saying. The speaker further explained that the closer the manager came to hitting this goal, the manager would have less of his or her pay cut.

Now, understand, this speaker was not talking about expanding the company's search geographically or reaching out to minority newspapers or other outlets to try and get more qualified minority candidates, which would have been great. I would encourage employers to do just that. What he was talking about was putting a goal in place where these managers had to hire a certain number or percentage of minorities into the organization within the next year ... or else!

"Oh ... My ... God!" I muttered to myself in astonishment.

I could not believe what I was hearing. Not only is such a plan highly illegal since it makes one's status as a minority *THE* major factor in hiring or promotion decisions and not *A* factor, as we just discussed, but this speaker's approach was certain to alienate the vast majority of White folks who hear his message. He has just destroyed any chance of getting any true buy-in from the organization's White employees, as well as many others.

Of course, since I was about the only White guy in the room, there didn't seem to be too much concern over this point.

As I looked around the room in horror, I saw many attendees hurriedly taking notes on what the speaker was saying. They loved his message and this approach. Why didn't anyone ever tell them about this brilliant plan before now?

(Probably because it is illegal.)

After the session, this guy was mobbed by the attendees asking for his card. He was a hit! The crowd loved his illegal message.

I, on the other hand, almost threw up.

The two HR people from the large Ohio company looked at me, laughed, and left. They did not come to this national HR conference to learn how to illegally increase the diversity at their facility.

This speaker was validating most every White person's worst fear regarding diversity and tolerance programs: *We want to boost the number of minority employees by illegally discriminating against White people and not making hiring decisions based on anyone's qualifications.*

It was the *Ricci* case all over again with competitive victimization supplying all the justification the speaker needed to break the law.

Unfortunately, there are way too many diversity experts who truly do have ulterior agendas, just as the city of New Haven did when it illegally discriminated against the Hispanic and White firefighters. This puts a stain on all the good work so many people really are doing in this field, but this type of programming happens a lot. However, I have not heard too many presenters come right out and announce their illegal plan to the world in such a blatant manner. It was like having some James Bond villain describe his evil plan to dominate the world before the bad guy then tries to kill him.

Again, at the most critical micro-level, it is all about jobs. And awarding jobs to people is a Zero-Sum game. If I give you a job, then I don't have that job to give to the next person.

Again, do you agree with this controversial statement that I made at the beginning of this book:

> **No one should ever be denied a job because of their demographics, such as race, color, religion, or sexual orientation.**
> **No one.**

I hope so. It is wrong, as well as illegal and unconstitutional, when it happens to Blacks, Asians, women, people with a different sexual orientation, and yes, even to White males. It is all wrong and it needs to stop.

The core reason most people get out of poverty is because they secured a good job. And yes, I realize how obvious that sounds. But think of it this way:

> When Jackie Robinson broke the color barrier in Major League Baseball and played first base for the Brooklyn Dodgers in 1947, the true issue was not that White players did not think Blacks were good enough to play with them. The issue was much more basic than that:
>
> > If a Black man could play first base ...
> > that meant that one White man would not.

It was about jobs. If Blacks could play baseball in the White leagues, then a lot of White baseball players would become unemployed. When it comes to bread and butter issues like employment, the situation becomes highly emotional and therefore dangerous and potentially violent very quickly.

Think about it: If White males actually support a traditional D&I program, could that program then be used to illegally limit their access to a better job? Will some illegal quota system be implemented, as this diversity expert was professing? (Clearly, this diversity expert had not been to law school.)

I say, "No." These so-called experts are wrong and no one should be discriminated against. It should not happen, and yes, I know it has happened to many Black qualified candidates in the past and it continues to this day. It is all wrong and should never be tolerated. In other words: Everyone should be upset whenever it happens to anyone.

Why? Because competitive victimization will fuel the fires of retaliation, which results in boomerang bigotry. This is truly everyone's problem.

In other words, "An eye for an eye just makes the whole world blind." (Mahatma Gandhi)

How Bad Is this Wave of Fear in White America?

Across the last 20 years, the Southern Poverty Law Center has tracked the number of hate groups in this country. In 1999, the Southern Poverty Law Center identified 452 active hate groups in America. However, by 2019, it was tracking 940 active hate groups, which is an increase of more than 100% ... and those are just the groups we know of and can track.[6]

If you want a real eye-opening experience, just take a look at the Southern Poverty Law Center's Hate Map. I have a hotlink to this map on my website at www.scottwarrick.com under the *Living The Five Skills of Tolerance* icon. You will never see the world, the United States, or the state where you live the same again.

Have you ever noticed the chants used by the White supremacists in the last several years: "You will not replace us?"

Whenever organizations ignore the law, this is one issue they are talking about.

Such illegal discrimination only fuels the far alt-right White supremacist organizations. This is why you see signs all over the country professing White Genocide. It is not true, but since it appeals to people's fears, it does not have to be true to be effective.

This is what CNN's Van Jones calls, "Whitelash."

Again, I think I am like most people. I want to be judged on my abilities, not my skin color. If the best thing I have ever done in my life is to be born White, then my life has been wasted.

Just like Ricci and the other firefighters who made tremendous sacrifices to better themselves and their careers, everyone should be given the chance to compete based on the skills they worked so hard to obtain, regardless of their personal demographics.

But then, as I was writing this particular chapter, I got a call from one of my clients who really wanted me to present my Five Skills of Tolerance program, but the board of directors insisted on getting someone who is Black. I cannot do anything about that.

Applying the Five Skills of Tolerance for Everyone

If you want to get real buy-in from the individual employees, then you need to address their micro-level issues, or their fears. In other words, you need to answer this question for your people:

> ## What is in it for me?

We must start focusing on providing life skills to everyone. We will not harass or discriminate against anyone. Instead, we will teach you how to make your lives better by teaching and adopting the Five Skills of Tolerance:

1. Develop Your Emotional Intelligence
2. Overcome Your Subconscious Brain & Resolve Conflict (EPR)
3. Identify & Stop Bullying
4. Understand Real Differences vs. Stereotypes
5. Don't Be an Enabler!

I will also tell employees point blank: I am not here to hurt you. I am here to help you. It is a whole new world today with cell phones. In a split second, you can do or say something really bad, which we have all done at some time in our lives. However, in today's world, someone will record you doing it, and that could be the end of you.

I will then ask them if that sounds like an exaggeration. Some will say, "Yes. You're being overdramatic."

I will then respond, "Then you must not watch the news very much. Has anyone ever heard of the 'Central Park Karen,' or Amy Cooper?"

I will then hear a collective moan come up from the audience.

I then explain that Christian Cooper, an avid birdwatcher and African American male, was bird watching on the morning of Monday, May 26, 2020 in the Ramble, a section of Central

Park that is full of winding paths and thick greenery that attracts over 230 different bird species.[7]

That is when he saw a dog off its leash.

"That's important to us birders because we know that dogs won't be off leash at all and we can go there to see the ground-dwelling birds," Christian Cooper said. "People spend a lot of money and time planting in those areas as well. Nothing grows in a dog run for a reason."[8]

At that same time, Amy Cooper was walking her unleashed dog, knowing it was against the rules.[9]

Christian Cooper said her dog was "tearing through the plantings," and he told Amy Cooper the dog needed to be on a leash. He was not yelling at Amy Cooper and he "was actually pretty calm."[10]

Christian Cooper then pulled out some dog treats. He told CNN he keeps dog treats with him to get dog owners to put their dogs on leashes because, in his experience, dog owners hate it when a stranger feeds their dog treats and immediately restrain their dogs to keep them from getting the treat.[11]

That is when Christian Cooper began recording. In the video, Amy Cooper can be seen dragging her dog by its collar to confront Christian Cooper. "Can you please stop? Sir, I'm asking you to stop [recording]," she said.[12]

"Please don't come close to me," Christian Cooper can be heard responding.

She then walked away from Christian Cooper and called the police, as she was still struggling to hold the dog by its collar. She told the police, "There is an African American man, I am in Central Park, he is recording me and threatening myself and my dog." [13]

This video instantly went viral. The next day, Amy Cooper's employer, Franklin Templeton, terminated her from her VP & Head of Investment Solutions position. The company wrote on Twitter, "We do not tolerate racism of any kind at Franklin Templeton."[14]

This exchange set off a firestorm for Amy Cooper, which included social media dubbing her the "Notorious Central Park Karen." Then, on Monday July 6, 2020, she was charged with filing a false police report that could have put her in jail for up to one year. Amy Cooper, 41, surrendered herself to the Manhattan DA's office. She was issued a desk appearance ticket and ordered to return to court on October 14, 2020 for her arraignment.[15]

Since then, Amy Cooper says that her entire life has been destroyed.[16] She lost her $170,000.00 a year job, as well as any real prospect of finding another one, her reputation has been obliterated, and even the dog she had with her in the park that day has been taken away from her.[17]

Interestingly enough, Amy Cooper could have easily been categorized as a left-winged liberal who did not see herself as having a bigoted bone in her body. It was reported that she voted for Barack Obama twice, she was a big fan of Hillary Clinton, and she donated money to both John Kerry and Pete Buttigieg. Still, when she was confronted by a Black bird watcher, she panicked and called in a false police report. It has destroyed her life.[18]

I always tell my audiences that I am convinced that if Amy Cooper had known about the Five Skills of Tolerance, this would not have happened to her. She would have known what was in her subconscious, so she could have rewired herself long before this incident occurred. She would have also known what to do in this highly stressful situation. I don't think it ever dawned on her that she was a human in the sense that she was naturally inclined to be a bullying, intolerant, bigoted, emotional child.

However, my goal is to see that this will never happen to you, regardless of your skin color, age, sexual orientation, and so on.

THAT is what is in all of this for you.

4

SKILL #1: DEVELOP YOUR EMOTIONAL INTELLIGENCE

What Does EMOTIONAL INTELLIGENCE Have to Do with TOLERANCE & DIVERSITY?

Whenever I present these materials in a seminar, I will often ask the audience: "Is it good to have diversity in an organization?"

I will then hear a resounding "Yes" from the audience.

I will then ask, "Really? Is it really?" The audience will then think about it for a few seconds.

I will then ask them, "Is it good to have older people and younger people working together?"

Again, I will always hear a resounding, "Yes!"

I will then ask, "Well, what do older people bring to the table?"

The audience will then say things like, "Experience!" "Been there ... Done that!" "Wisdom!"

I will then follow up with, "And what do younger people bring to the organization?"

The audience will then respond by saying things like, "Energy!" "Technology!" "New ideas!"

I will then ask the audience, "And so, you think it is good to put these people together, right?"

They will then inevitably respond by shouting, "Oh, yes! That would really help an organization out!"

I will then lean into the audience and ask, "Really? Do you really think it is a good idea to put these people together who view the world in such very different ways?"

The audience will think about it for a second before I ask, "And what is going to happen the first time that young whipper-snapper tells that older, more experienced person that he is *wrong*?"

The audience will think about that for a second. Most people will smile, thinking of the inevitable clash of egos that is going to occur. I will then ask them, "And what is going to happen the first time an older more experienced person tells that young pompous college graduate that she is *wrong*?"

The audience usually laughs out loud as they see the destructive nature of intolerance and immaturity starting to rear its ugly head. That is where our diversity, or our Diversity of Ideas, works against us. In other words, we are very tolerant people ... as long as everyone agrees with us.

Is having diversity in an organization, which results in a Diversity of Ideas, good? Yes ... *IF* you are smart enough to use it, which means controlling your ego and emotions long enough to listen to someone else's ideas, which is tolerance ... especially when that other person disagrees with you.

THAT is when our Diversity of Ideas works.

The premise of diversity is actually pretty simple:

> **Diversity is anything that makes us different from one another.**

That is it. Simple.

In fact, if we put 50 White Anglo-Saxon Protestant straight males into a room together, it wouldn't look like we had much diversity.

But think about it: How long would it be until they disagreed with one another and were at each other's throats?

If you need a real-life example, just think of Congress about 30 years ago.

Black people don't hate White people because of their skin color and vice versa. Likewise, older people don't hate younger people because of their age, straight people don't hate gays because of their sexual orientation, and so on and so on. People hate each other because they *think* differently from each other. Someone dared to disagree with them on some highly emotional issue, which stepped on their ego and caused their emotions to burst out of control.

The issue here is really simple:

- First ... you don't train people in DIVERSITY. Diversity is a noun. Diversity is what you *ARE* ... not what you *DO*. We have diversity ... we need to become tolerant. I never try to teach people how to be White. That is ridiculous, even though I have decades of experience in being a White guy. Yes, I am an expert at being White.

- You train people to be TOLERANT. To be tolerant is a verb. You train people in the skills they need to be tolerant of anyone who is different from them. It is vital that we are all on the same page and have the same definition of what I am talking about when I use the term tolerance. In short, tolerance means:

> **I am not going to persecute or bully you because you are different.**

Again, it is simple.

Simply having a diverse environment is not enough. Surrounding ourselves with people whose ideas differ from ours will end in disaster if a culture of tolerance, where it is safe to speak up, is not fostered. That means we must have emotionally intelligent people on board who are tolerant of other people's differences and different opinions. That is our ultimate goal: To build TRUST, which asks, "Is It SAFE?"

Every organization needs to strive to attain and maintain a safe environment. That means:

- Is the environment safe from germs in the middle of a pandemic?
- Will I go home with all my fingers and toes?
- Is it safe to be different, like being Black, female, gay, and so on?
- Is it safe to disagree with other people?
- Is it safe to disagree with my boss?

That is the litmus test for any environment: Is it safe?

If not, then the organization will likely be toxic.

That is why I am not a big fan of employee surveys. I will often talk to organizations that are thinking of paying a consulting agency a lot of money to conduct one for them. My client will typically show me the website of the consulting company that is proposing the survey, and I must say, the employees on the website always look really happy after they took the survey. So, it must work, right? I mean, marketing people wouldn't lie, would they?

After listening for a while to how thorough this survey is and how professional these consultants are, I always ask the same question: "Why don't you just go out and talk to the employees and ask them first-hand what they think of the place?"

I will then always get a chuckle or a laugh from my client as they reply, "Well, they are not going to tell us the truth."

"Why not?" I will ask.

"Because they are afraid if they say the wrong thing they will get in trouble!" I am always told.

"So, let me make sure I've got this," I will reply, using my best set of Parroting skills. "They won't tell you the truth because they don't think it is safe to speak up. Right?"

"Of course not," I am always told. "That is why the survey is anonymous."

To that, I always respond, "And that is your root problem. You don't need an employee survey to tell you what is wrong. There is no trust here because it is not safe. People have learned if they say the wrong thing that someone, probably a supervisor, will attack them or they will get stabbed in the back later."

That is the role emotional intelligence and tolerance plays in an organization: To make it safe, which builds real trust.

For example, I once had a client who employed a small number of minorities. This kept the company from securing several government contracts. So, the company hired a human resource and diversity expert to help them solve this problem. The consultant told the company it needed to become more diverse. He told the company it had to hire more qualified minorities, such as more qualified Blacks, Hispanics, and so on.

The company understood the logic of what the consultant was saying, so it got right to work looking for more qualified minorities. The company actually implemented the perfect D&I recruiting program. It widened its recruiting scope so it would get as many resumes as possible and within a year, the organization hired many qualified minorities. No one was terminated to make room for these minority employees. Instead, for all its open positions, it conducted a fair and comprehensive search for the right person, regardless of minority status. They even found a great candidate from Myanmar, which was unusual for that area.

It had truly become a diverse organization and it was able to hire employees who were more qualified and better workers than they had ever gotten before in their history. To celebrate this achievement, the company hung a large world map in the lunchroom and put a pin in each country where an employee was born, including various parts of the United States. It looked like a map of the U.N.

In the end, the whole plan was a disaster.

A disaster? Why? I mean, everything sounded so good ... on paper. I would have thought this story was going to have a happy ending. Well, not really.

Even though the company did a fantastic job in recruiting the best people it could regardless of demographics, the consultant failed to tell the organization that it needed to double up its efforts on addressing the emotional intelligence and the tolerance level of the organization's current employees, as well as the new ones coming aboard. The consultant focused entirely on increasing the company's diversity, which was a good thing. But failing to also address the intolerance of its people would be their undoing, which I saw as malpractice on the part of the consultant.

I think they all forgot they were dealing with humans.

Now, I know we are just getting started in this book, but I would bet all of you lunch that most of you are probably thinking that the old White guys were the ones who were harassing and discriminating against the new Black employees. Well, you would be partly right.

However, the company ran into some other tolerance issues that never occurred to them. For instance, the company learned very quickly that the new employees who were Black but were actually born and raised in Africa made it very clear to the African American employees that they were not really Africans. Now, if you want to see some real workplace violence, throw that little tidbit out there at lunch. (Again, insert a little more sarcasm here.)

Also, the company already had a few employees working there who were gay. Naturally, some of the newer employees tried to convert their homosexual counterparts to Christianity and save them from their inevitable trip into eternal Hell. I mean, they were just trying to help them out, right?

And, of course, we did have the company's old guard still working there who now didn't even have to leave the building to find someone to hate.

Within two years, the company had several civil rights charges pending, a workplace violence incident, and a couple of full-blown lawsuits.

But then, diversity, and all the various ideas that come with it, is a good thing ... right?

In short, it was not safe to speak up, so eventually, no one did. Trust was destroyed, which killed every program the organization tried to implement.

Emotional children have very fragile egos and cannot control their emotions. The great American-Muslim philosopher, David Khari Webber Chappelle, describes these emotional children as having a "brittle spirit." That is exactly right.

It truly is a struggle for most humans to admit that they might be wrong or that they just learned something new. That type of immature mindset will destroy the trust in any relationship because it proves that it is not safe to voice your own opinion.

Without emotionally intelligent people dominating the organization and directing the culture, conflicts do not get resolved. Instead, the culture allows us to crucify anyone who dares to disagree with us, so it is not safe to be different or voice your opinion. It is not safe to go to work. Any degree of trust that might have existed in the organization dies.

> **Emotional Intelligence gives us the skill of self-control that enables us to be more tolerant.**

What Is Tolerance?

Again, as in any program, you must define your terms. If not, everyone will look at your program in a different way, which is not good. In fact, if we asked 100 people to define the term tolerance, we would walk away with many definitions, and many would not even be close to what I mean in this program.

For this program, tolerance means: *We are not going to persecute or bully someone because they are different.*

That is it. Simple.

> **The *ACT* of tolerance comes from the *MINDSET* of emotional intelligence.**

For any program to be a success, it is critical that its concepts are simple. The simpler the better. Otherwise, how will you effectively communicate it to everyone across your entire organization? It is a lot like playing telephone. If you whisper something into one person's ear, who then whispers it to the next person and so on, the message will get lost by the time it reaches the third or fourth person unless the message is sickeningly simple. Remember: Simple is brilliant.

When I refer to being tolerant, I am *not* talking about how you think. I am not addressing your mindset.

Being tolerant of others also does not mean that you are going to look down on someone or simply put up with others. That would actually be very intolerant because you would be persecuting or bullying that person. That type of bullying behavior is not allowed. There has to be coaching and consequences for those who bully others. That is called leadership.

However, with tolerance, I am talking about governing the way you act ... the way you behave.

Still, I will often get complaints over using the word "tolerance." I will hear such comments as: "I don't want to be tolerated. I want to be accepted or appreciated."

My response to this question is always the same: Do you really think that we have the right to tell you and your co-workers how to think?

I usually get a stunned look from the person, so I ask, "Wouldn't that make us more than just a little intolerant?"

This is one reason why the word "tolerance" is used by the Southern Poverty Law Center, by the EEOC in its 2016 *Select Task Force on the Study of Harassment in the Workplace* report, and by so many successful bullying programs across this country. It is alright to tell people how to behave. It is not alright to tell them how to think.

Even more importantly, tolerance is the term used by the United States Supreme Court. The Supreme Court has stressed in no uncertain terms that being tolerant, which means controlling how we act towards others, is most definitely regulated by our laws. In fact, some of the circuit courts have even come right out and said that the law is not telling anyone how to think, which is acceptance. However, the law is certainly telling Americans how to act, which is tolerance.

The difference between acceptance and tolerance is immense. An organization cannot, and should not, require its people to change their beliefs. Of course, if an organization's Five Skills of Tolerance program can get someone to re-evaluate their beliefs and become more accepting of others, then more power to them. Education has the power to do just that. Education can change people's attitudes and build acceptance. It is a vital part of our rewiring process, as we will discuss later.

Many times over, I have seen every day ordinary bigots become much more accepting of others, but it was not done by requiring them to do it. That only fosters more resistance.

I think so many diversity leaders try but fail to get others to be accepting or to appreciate the differences of others because they are simply using the wrong tool. They are trying to use a hammer where a screwdriver is needed. They are trying to force others to change the way they think instead of focusing on the neurological aspects of the subconscious brain, which is where our implicit biases reside. Changing the way people think is done by rewiring their subconscious brain. If diversity experts understood more about how the human brain works, I think they would stop trying to force people to think a certain way, but they would instead start showing them how to think in a different way.

That is how Frank Meeink, a hard-core Skinhead, changed the way he thought, which is how he became accepting of those he used to persecute. You can never order a Skinhead to accept other people, but you can rewire how they think. There is a world of difference between these two methodologies. We will discuss in more detail how Frank managed to become more accepting of others in Chapter 6 *SKILL#3: Identify & Stop Bullying*. We will also discuss exactly how we can all rewire our subconscious brains in much greater detail in Chapter 5 *SKILL #2: Overcome Your Subconscious Brain & Resolve Conflict (EPR)*.

Rewiring the subconscious brain is how you gain acceptance for other people, not by ordering someone to do it.

Unfortunately, requiring employees to be accepting of others is the message that has permeated throughout the diversity community for years. Actually, some of the most intolerant people I have ever had the misfortune of meeting have been at diversity conferences. This is because too many people let their emotions control them and they end up going on an intolerant Blues Brothers' "Mission from God" quest, much like what happened during the Inquisition. Since they believe their cause is just, they also tend to believe that the end justifies the means. They often believe that telling others how to think is just fine. It is all very Machiavellian because they believe their cause is pure. Many of them intend to change the world by making you become more accepting of others. In other words, you will either adopt my beliefs or get fired.

Again, I respectfully disagree.

I don't believe any employer has the right to tell their employees what to believe or how to think. Requiring acceptance actually destroys the ideas of both tolerance and diversity.

- If everyone thought and believed the same things, then where is the diversity?
- If we require everyone to believe a certain way, then where is the tolerance for other people's ideas?

Employers do not have the right to tell a Christian fundamentalist to be accepting of Satanists. They do not have the right to tell Jewish people they have to be accepting of Allah. No one has the right to tell a Muslim they have to be accepting of homosexuals. No one has this right.

However, an employer has every right, and a legal duty, to tell employees how to behave, both on and off the job in many jurisdictions. It should be a disciplinary offense to persecute or bully anyone, regardless of the reason. That needs to be a staple of every culture.

Years ago, I got a real lesson in the tremendous difference between tolerance and acceptance. One of my clients settled a large harassment lawsuit and as part of the settlement agreement, they had to adopt a new diversity program. They were also ordered to give their employees three hours of training in diversity every year for the next five years.

In the training sessions that all the employees had to attend, the diversity expert told everyone that the company was establishing a brand new culture. As part of this new culture, everyone would be required to be accepting of each other's differences.

After each session, the employees had to sign a statement saying they would be accepting of the differences of everyone around them. Now, on the surface, this sounded great. Most people signed the document and approved of the direction the organization was going.

However, a small group of Muslim men, six altogether, refused to sign the document. The trainer talked to them, as did their manager and the HR director. However, these men all remained steadfast. They would not sign this paper.

It was at this point that I got a call from the company.

I met with all six men together in the conference room. Since this was a conflict situation, I first assumed my signature conflict resolution stance: I leaned back in my chair, folded my hands across my chest and cocked my head a bit to the right. I got into my best posture of being calm and relaxed, a necessity when practicing EPR.

I started with my Empathic Listening by asking, "Who wants to tell me what is going on?"

After I asked the question, I just relaxed and shut up. It was not time for me to talk. I needed to listen to these men and understand their point of view, not mine. That is **Empathic Listening.**

One man started by telling me that in their religion, Islam, homosexuality is a mortal sin. They are not to engage in it, sanction it, or approve of it in any way. If they do, then they will go to Hell.

Another man chimed in and added that if they signed this piece of paper, they would be admitting that they are accepting of the homosexuals working at this organization. As a result, they would all later burn in Hell.

Just to make sure I understood everything they were telling me, I continued using my EPR skills. I Parroted back everything they told me to make sure I understood. We were not going to move ahead in this conflict until I repeated everything back to them to their satisfaction.

I asked them point blank, "Now, let me make sure I've got this. You're telling me that because this paper says you are going to be accepting of everyone's differences, and since there are people working here who are homosexual, you will go to Hell if you sign this paper because you will be saying that you are accepting of homosexuality. Is that right?"

"Yes, yes! That is right," they all responded together, nodding their heads.

I understood exactly what they were saying. I remember thinking, "Now, that is a heck of a choice, isn't it? Getting fired, which is bad, or burning in Hell for all of eternity, which is really bad. That is why they call it Hell. It is really bad."

In this case, I agreed with them. They changed my mind. As part of my EPR system, I did not have to give them what I call a "Reward." You only give someone a "Reward" when you are going to disagree with the other person in order to validate their right to their opinion. If that was the case, I would have said something like, "I see where you are coming from, but what about this?" This is the reward that is worth more than money: Validating your right to your opinion, which shows that it is safe to disagree with me and builds trust.

People rarely get angry with you when you agree with them. They get angry when you disagree with them. That is why you give someone a "Reward" whenever you disagree with another person. It is important to let them know that it is OK to have a different opinion. It builds trust because you are showing them that it is safe to disagree with you.

This is why the only time we ever build real trust with others is when we are in conflict with them. Again, since trust means that it is safe to disagree with someone else, you really are never too sure if it is alright to disagree with another person until you have actually done it. That is why we've all had relationships with others for years, but we are not too sure if we really trust them because we have never proven to each other that it is safe to disagree. However, once you do show that it is safe, then you are starting to build trust.

In other words, handling conflicts in the right way helps to strengthen your relationships with others, and you do that by controlling your emotions and ego (or first base), and then using your EPR skills to address the conflict (or second base).

But in this case, I told them I agreed with them. I told them the company does not have a right to tell them how to think, but it does have a right, and an obligation, to tell them how to behave.

So, I asked them, "Would you be willing to sign a document that said you would be tolerant of anyone who is different from you? That you would not persecute or bully anyone who is different?"

"Oh, yeah," they all instantly replied. "We would sign that today."

One man told me, "We actually like many of the homosexuals working here. It is really a shame they're all going to burn in Hell."

"Yes," I agreed. "That's going to be rough."

All six men agreed to sign a newly worded document that used the term "tolerant" rather than "acceptance."

Again, I have been attacked on this issue of tolerance vs. acceptance more times than I can count. I have had people get up and storm out of my session at national diversity conferences when I address this issue. I have had people openly yell at me in my sessions and between sessions at diversity conferences that employees must be accepting of their differences or they cannot work at that organization. I actually had a Fortune 500 clothing retailer openly tell me that if someone did not agree with the organization's Christian beliefs, that those people could not work there.

"But you are not a church. You are a retailer. That is not only wrong, but it is highly illegal," I told them.

"We don't care. You have to accept our values or you can't work here," they told me.

I never presented for that organization again. It is clearly one of the most bigoted organizations I have ever met.

A D&I program should never be used to further anyone's personal crusade, agenda, or to force someone else's beliefs onto others. Isn't that interesting? Many people love the idea of having diversity, until you refuse to accept their beliefs. Then, they want to discriminate against you because you think differently. That is not diversity. It is Fascism, which is the "forcible suppression of opposition" (*Dictionary.com*). That is also the very definition of intolerance.

Again, if you are going to get punched in the face, do you really care if the blow comes from the left or the right?

Of course, I have never met a diversity person who wants to be seen as meeting these definitions, but sometimes our zeal to "do the right thing" leads us down this path. Ordering others to think a certain way only forces others to rebel, just like the proverbial punching bag.

D&I programs should be for everyone of all beliefs, colors, races, religions, gender, sexual orientation, and so on. That is why I absolutely demand and enforce a culture where everyone must be tolerant of others and their beliefs. We will not bully you because you look different, sound different, or think different from others.

Also, this standard of tolerance is the lowest I have ever seen ... and we cannot even hit that. If we truly were tolerant people, there would be no need for Affirmative Action Plans, much less illegal quota systems, because we would always hire the best person for the job. We would hire the Jamaal's of the world as often as we hire the Johnny's. We would not harass and bully women because they are female. We would promote the gay male as often as we promote the straight males. There would be peace in the Middle East, and there would be no more shootings in our schools, and so on.

Yes, as low as the tolerance standard is, we cannot even hit that, which is why you see the state America and the world are in today.

So, how are you ever going to make everyone be tolerant of others? An organization's message should be very clear on this point: If you cannot meet this minimum standard of tolerance, then you will need to leave. Intolerant behavior will not be tolerated. In other words ...

> **We will be very intolerant
> of your intolerance.**

NASA: A Case Study of Intolerance

Yes, even if an organization is filled with more geniuses per square inch than any other organization in the world, it cannot function if emotional children are running it.

Many people are surprised to discover that the Challenger and Columbia disasters did not occur *solely* because of technical problems. Instead, they were both caused by intolerance.

Yes, emotional children were running NASA.

Long before Challenger launched on January 28, 1986, several NASA employees noticed there was a problem with the shuttle's O-rings. Many of these NASA employees spoke up and brought this issue to management's attention. Some wrote reports outlining precisely what was wrong with these O-rings on the Challenger Space Shuttle. These reports specifically said if these O-rings were not replaced, there was a high probability they would fail if it was launched in temperatures of less than 56 degrees Fahrenheit. That means the space shuttle would likely explode on take-off.[19]

For those of you who are not rocket engineers, the O-rings act like the gaskets in your car's engine. The gaskets in your engine keep the fluid from leaking out all over the place when the car is running. That is what the O-rings on Challenger were supposed to do: They kept the rocket fuel from leaking out all over the rocket boosters.

However, since the O-rings on Challenger were getting old, they were becoming brittle and inflexible. When the temperature dropped, the O-rings lost even more of their elasticity. In cold temperatures, they would shrink so much they would not be able to keep the rocket fuel from leaking onto the outside of the shuttle. Since Challenger generates thousands of degrees of heat on take-off, this made for a deadly situation for the seven astronauts onboard.[20]

Now, you could understand that hearing such vital but disturbing news from NASA's rocket engineers would be hard for management to take. Such a revelation would delay flight schedules and cost tens of millions of dollars to correct. As upsetting as this news would be to NASA officials, you would also think they would want to act upon it quickly. However, instead of correcting these critical issues, NASA simply ignored this information.[21]

Not only did the leadership at NASA fail to address the problem, but some NASA engineers were fired for speaking up.[22]

Instantly, trust was destroyed. NASA proved to everyone that it was not safe to speak up. Right up to the day before Challenger launched, Roger Boisjoly, an engineer with Morton Thiokol and a subcontractor at NASA, was screaming and yelling at the team of engineers and managers who were debating whether to give NASA the go ahead to launch the next day. Boisjoly told the NASA team that Challenger would explode because the O-rings on the fuel tanks needed to be replaced. Boisjoly even showed this team photographs of the Discovery Space Shuttle where the O-rings started to fail on its flight in the previous year. These photographs showed that the O-rings on Discovery came within 1 millimeter of burning through and releasing the fuel onto the outside of the shuttle. NASA had dodged a bullet with Discovery, and Boisjoly was convinced NASA would not be so lucky with Challenger.[23]

At this point Boisjoly was told to take off his engineering hat and put on his management hat. The Morton Thiokol team then voted to recommend that NASA launch Challenger the next day. Even though NASA leadership knew all about the problems the shuttle was having with these O-rings, NASA's leadership accepted the recommendation to launch.[24]

Boisjoly went home that night and told his wife, "They are going to launch tomorrow and kill the astronauts. You would have to be blind, deaf and dumb to ignore this."[25]

That next morning, January 28, 1986, Challenger was covered in icicles over one meter long. The temperature that morning was not 56 degrees Fahrenheit, which was the temperature that NASA feared the O-rings would fail, but it was actually 36 degrees Fahrenheit. Challenger exploded 73 seconds after launch.[26]

Not only did seven astronauts lose their lives, but the trust throughout the organization was shot.

In short: Even when lives were at stake, it was not safe to speak up at NASA.[27]

Very few NASA employees would speak up after the Challenger disaster because they feared what management would do to them. They saw their colleagues get fired for speaking up, so they were naturally afraid of management's reprisal if they brought up any issues contrary to what NASA brass wanted to hear. NASA management had proven that it could not be trusted. [27]

William Rogers, a former U.S. Secretary of State under President Nixon and the U.S. Attorney General under President Eisenhower, was chosen to lead the investigation into the Challenger disaster. The *Report of the Presidential Commission on the Space Shuttle Challenger Accident*, more commonly referred to as the *Rogers Commission Report*, was extremely critical of NASA's administration.

The Rogers Commission found that NASA was blinded by its "can-do" attitude. Since the space shuttle program was so strapped by schedule pressures and budget shortages, spare parts had to be cannibalized from one vehicle to launch another. The Rogers Report cited "gross mismanagement" as being the primary reason why Challenger exploded.[28]

In the end, NASA had fostered and promoted a culture that was very intolerant of anyone who voiced a contrary opinion. Again, it was not safe to speak up at NASA, so there was no trust.[29]

Boisjoly later resigned and suffered a nervous breakdown. However, the NASA official who failed to heed the warnings of his own engineers, who accepted Morton Thiokol's recommendation without asking any questions and who ordered the launch, was later promoted.[30]

Still, the culture at NASA did not change. ... even after it blew up seven astronauts.

Interestingly, after I presented this program to one of my clients, I got a real treat. One employee came up to me afterwards and said, "You know, my father retired from NASA."

I responded by saying, "Really. Was he there during Challenger?"

"Oh, yes," she responded. "Actually, that was why he retired. He was so disgusted over how NASA handled the problem with the O-rings that he just couldn't work there anymore. Everyone knew that these O-rings were bad. Everyone. It was only a matter of time before it blew up. It was common knowledge."

Seventeen years later, on January 16, 2003, the Columbia Space Shuttle launched. However, some engineers at NASA noticed when Columbia took off, an unusually large piece of the shuttle's heat shield broke loose and struck the left wing. When this piece of rock-hard heat shield struck the left wing, it appeared to explode on contact. This alarmed many of NASA's engineers.[31]

Since Columbia's launch was videotaped, the NASA engineers reviewed the tape again and again. After viewing the tape several times, many of NASA's engineers thought that this piece of the heat shield might have put a hole in the left wing.[32]

To understand how serious this situation was to the NASA engineers, it is important to know a little bit about rocket science. When any space shuttle is re-entering earth's atmosphere, it is traveling at about 17,500 miles per hour. This will generate temperatures on the exterior of the space shuttle over 8,000 degrees Fahrenheit.[33]

Since all of the heat shield is located on the outside of the space shuttle, Columbia would have no protection from this intense heat when it tries to re-enter the earth's atmosphere if there is a hole in the left wing. So, 8,000 degrees of super-heated gasses would enter the space shuttle through this hole, which would cook the astronauts alive and then explode.[34]

This is a horrifying scenario by anyone's standards.

The NASA engineers asked for permission to have the astronauts take a digital photograph of the wing the next time they went out on a spacewalk to see if Columbia was still safe to re-enter the earth's atmosphere.[35]

NASA management not only refused this request, but it actively prevented anyone from having any photos taken of the left wing to see if it had been damaged on take-off. Why would NASA's management refuse to let the astronauts photograph the left wing to see if it was damaged? Because any further investigations could delay completing the International Space Station on time. So, the photo was never taken.[36]

And, of course, on February 1, 2003, Columbia tried to re-enter the earth's atmosphere. Since there was a hole in the left wing, all 8,000 degrees of super-heated gasses entered Columbia causing it to explode and kill another seven astronauts.[37]

After the Columbia disaster, investigators confirmed what the NASA engineers thought all along. The piece of heat shield that broke loose from the shuttle on take-off had put a hole in the left wing of Columbia about 10 inches in diameter. As a result, when Columbia made its re-entry, much of this intense heat entered the shuttle, causing it to explode and killing everyone on board.[38]

Four Star Admiral Hal Gehman was appointed by President Bush to oversee the Columbia Accident Investigation Board, or the CAIB. The final conclusions of the board were released on August 26, 2003. Again, just as the Rogers Commission found that "gross mismanagement" by the NASA leadership caused the Challenger disaster, this report on the Columbia disaster was highly critical of NASA management, which basically said: "NASA's management system is not safe to run this program."[39]

Exactly how many people do you have to kill before you change what you are doing? Cleary, NASA failed to learn anything from the lessons of Challenger. The CAIB reported that

NASA still had the same egotistical "can-do-at-all-costs" attitude that caused the Challenger disaster. Anyone who voiced a contrary opinion was punished in some way, which included termination. NASA still had a culture that was very intolerant of anyone who voiced a contrary opinion.[40]

Again, it was not safe to speak up, so there was no trust.

NASA officials were simply more concerned with money and meeting its precious schedule than saving the lives of the astronauts on Challenger and Columbia.[41]

According to Admiral Gehman, had NASA management allowed its engineering team to take a digital photograph of the outside of Columbia's left wing, they would have seen the 10-inch gaping hole caused by the piece of heat shield that broke loose on takeoff. NASA could have then delayed Columbia's re-entry and possibly sent another space shuttle up into space to rescue the seven Columbia astronauts. In Admiral Gehman's words, "They would have done something" to save the astronauts. Tragically, NASA engineers were never given a chance to try.[42]

After receiving these results, Sean O'Keefe, the Administrator of NASA, said in a nationally televised press conference: "We get it."[43]

What Mr. O'Keefe explained was that NASA recognized that it needed to fix its culture.[44]

It is very interesting that back in the 1960s and 1970s, when the space program was using technology that was far inferior to what NASA was using with Challenger and Columbia, we never lost one astronaut in flight. Not one American astronaut died in space. Not one.

Today, using technology far superior to what NASA had at its disposal in the 1960s and 1970s, NASA has killed fourteen people in flight. Fourteen.

Are they smart at NASA? Think about it: They really are rocket scientists. NASA employs some of the world's top geniuses. Unfortunately, that is even more reason people get too big for their britches. It is not an issue of IQ.

Instead, it is an issue of emotional intelligence, or Emotional Quotient, or EQ. Emotional children are very intolerant of others. They have a brittle spirit. It is not safe to disagree with an emotional child, so there is no trust.

In fact, NASA's problem was clear: NASA was being run by bullying, intolerant, bigoted, emotional children.

This is why really, really smart people do really, really stupid things.

Remember: Just like everything else, having a high IQ, believe it or not, also has a downside. Today, we know that as our IQ rises, as our titles increase, as the number of degrees we hold increases, as our time on the job increases, and anything else that boosts our ego too much ... *Our Emotional Intelligence Tends To Drop Like A Rock.*[15]

If you want to see if uncontrolled ego was really the problem at NASA, ask yourself these questions:

- Would the NASA executives still have terminated the NASA employees who spoke up about the O-ring defects on Challenger if *their* family members were on the space shuttle?

- Would NASA management have allowed its engineers to have digital photographs taken of the left wing on Columbia and examine the situation more closely before it made its re-entry if one of *their* family members were on board?

Ego quickly gets put into perspective when it is your butt that is on the line.

Fixing the Problem:
NASA'S Tolerance/Diversity Program

In 2007, I heard Sharon Wong, the Special Assistant for Diversity at NASA, speak at the Society for Human Resource Management's National Diversity Conference in Philadelphia, Pennsylvania. Ms. Wong's topic was *Making Space for Everyone: The Diversity Journal at NASA Goddard.*[46]

Ms. Wong explained that NASA now wanted to create a culture where employees would feel safe to speak up whenever they felt an issue needed to be addressed.[47] NASA wanted to create a tolerant environment where it was safe to be different, which included speaking up.

In February 2004, NASA started its *Can We Talk: A Dialogue with the Center Director* program. This program provided "an informal dialogue session with either the Center Director or the Deputy Director." There was no agenda set for these meetings and no set topics. Instead, it was established as "an opportunity for employees to tell the Center's leadership what's on their minds."[48]

NASA employees were also specifically told:

> "Emphasis is placed on enhancing personal growth and effectiveness throughout the process of listening, introspection, finding meaning, and building acceptance for differing perspectives."[49]

Emotional intelligence and tolerance were required. Again and again, NASA reinforced to everyone that it was safe to speak up in this new environment. That is practically the textbook definition of trust.

NASA's Diversity Program became part of its Strategic Mission. For instance, the principles of tolerance taught in this program would also become part of NASA's overall Performance Plan. Every employee would be rated on their performance reviews regarding how well they practice these principles.

NASA also established a 180-degree feedback program so employees and management alike could let each other know how they were doing in upholding these principles of tolerance.

In the end, NASA promised to change its culture to one where employees would be tolerant of others when they disagreed with one another ... and it did. The culture today is one where contrary opinions are welcomed. If someone has an issue, the culture requires that it be safe to speak up. Today, NASA is a very different organization from the one that launched Challenger and Columbia.

NASA built this level of trust by proving to their employees it was safe to speak up. Telling the employees they could trust NASA management accomplished nothing. However, allowing employees to speak their minds, and then rewarding them when they did, proved to everyone that it was safe to be different, which includes speaking up. That builds trust.

Remember: No one believes anything you say. They watch what you do.

In 2010, I got another real treat. I was presenting this program in Cleveland, Ohio and someone from NASA's John Glenn Research Center was in the audience. When I got to this section regarding NASA, I asked her how the culture has changed at NASA in the last few years. She replied that the culture had changed remarkably. She told me it is simply a whole new culture ... one that is much better than before. She said she actually enjoys going into work now.

> **THAT is the power of emotional intelligence and tolerance.**

5

SKILL #2: OVERCOME YOUR SUBCONSCIOUS BRAIN & RESOLVE CONFLICT (EPR)

The Human Genome

When I was a little White boy, I did what all good little Methodists do: I went to church. Now, church was pretty boring for me. The minister collected some money from everyone, we would sing about it, and then he would preach on something that only the adults could relate to, except for my Grandpa, who would close his eyes and meditate while all of this was going on. I thought for sure I would get a good seat in heaven because I had already had the Hell bored right out of me.

However, the story of Adam and Eve always stuck with me. The idea that these two people were doing a pre-historic version of *Naked and Afraid* boggled my mind. Here were two people living in Eden, naked, and they didn't know it. They did not even have to work too hard. It was truly perfect.

This was one thing the Muslins, Jews, and Christians could all agree on. For the first few hundred years or so, it was OK to date your cousins, much like the royal family still does today.

If you really thought about it, we are all somehow related to one another.

Of course, these were all just my beliefs. To think that two people could actually start a family tree that would result in over seven billion people living on the planet was probably not realistic. Surely, the story of Adam and Eve had to be one of those Bible myths that sounded good, but it was not really true.

Until 2003 ...

In 1990, the Human Genome Project was launched. The Human Genome Project was an international scientific research project whose goal was to determine the base pair that makes up human DNA, and then identify and map the human genome.[50]

Most of the government-sponsored sequencing in this project was performed in twenty universities and research centers in the United States, the United Kingdom, France, Japan, Germany, and China.[51]

The project was finally completed on April 14, 2003 with some remarkable findings. To this day, it remains the world's largest collaborative biological project ever undertaken.[52]

One of the most interesting findings of the project was the Eve conclusion: That Eve was indeed the "Mother of All Humans."[53] According to the Human Genome Project, and even newer research conducted by Peter Ralph of the University of Southern California Dornsife, we now know that the Bible was right all along:

> **Everyone on Earth is related to everyone else.**[54]

In more general terms, we are all basically cousins with one another, probably about 50 times removed at the most.

This means we are all part of the same tribe. We are all part of the same team. There should not be any "out" group. We are all part of the "in" group family. We are all human beings together, so we actually have more in common with each other than differences. [55]

Of course, I thought the next most important question to ask at that point was, "Where was Eden?" Where was this great place that had everything anyone would ever want ... this great land of milk, honey, and Reese's cups? I assumed it had to be someplace like Hawaii, Costa Rica, or the Caribbean. Someplace with a beach.

Well, believe it or not, it was in east Africa.[56]

"Oh, my God," I thought to myself. East Africa? Really? Are you kidding me? Eden was in Africa? That could not be true. I mean, it is like Africa hot there. I could not imagine my lily-White skin living in east Africa. I would get skin cancer and be dead within the week.

As I continued my research, I came across a few other little tidbits of handy information. Adam and Eve not only lived in east Africa, but they were Black.[57]

Now, that got my attention, and it was not something they taught me at my all-White Methodist church. Everyone I know, including myself, all come from Black people. Really?

But then, that does explain a lot about human migration and human behavior.

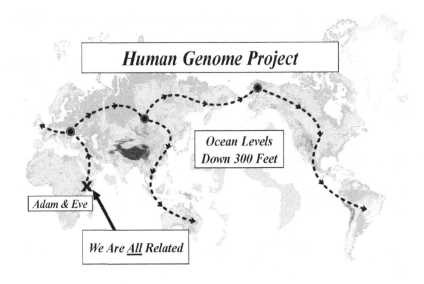

As it turns out, the first people on this planet had dark skin. This was necessary due to the hot African sun. As my ancestors inbred with each other more and more, some of us must have thought it was a bad idea to stay in Africa. I mean, it was just too hot.

Some of my more direct ancestors traveled north, where it was cooler. Some of my relatives stayed in the Middle East. Their bodies decided that they did not need that much melanin anymore, so their skin lightened up a bit. My more direct relatives thought it was still too hot to stay in the Middle East, so they went further north and made a left. They traveled across Europe until they ran out of land. They probably stayed there for a while until they got sick of the French. They then probably made a boat and paddled their way over to England. However, after a few years of that, my relatives probably thought the Brits were a little too snooty, so they made another boat and paddled their way over to County Cork, Ireland. This is where we basically drank for the next few years. Then, in the 1840's, some kind of fungus made the potatoes go bad. It was either starve, eat each other, or go to America. We decided we would try going to America first. We traveled to the United States where we arrived just in time to get shot and killed in the Civil War. Welcome to America!

My wife's family, on the other hand, also left Africa and traveled north. However, at one point, her family made a right hand turn instead of a left. Her family became what we now call Russians. When the Russian Revolution came, being Jewish and all, they decided it was time to get away from the Bolsheviks. Again, that meant coming to the United States in the middle of World War I, just in time to get sent back to Europe to kill some Germans.

So, the Bible was right, with a few little twists.

This revelation is important for a few reasons.

First, it shows how silly our prejudices are in this world. When you hate someone just because they are different from you, you are hating your own brother, cousin, and so on. That is not just philosophical; that is a scientific and Biblical fact.

This Human Genealogy also explains why all humans are neurologically hard-wired the same.

The Neurology of Us

As I wrote in my book, *Solve Employee Problems Before They Start: Resolving Conflict In The Real World,* I explained in great detail how all humans are wired the same. Men, women, Whites, Blacks, Asians, Hispanics, Jews, and Methodists are all wired neurologically to be human.

Unfortunately, we all share the same wiring that instantly triggers us to go into a fight or flight response whenever we sense danger. That was fine 5,000 years ago when Fred Flintstone spent his days either hunting for food or trying not to become something else's food. This system of fight or flight was able to kick Fred's emotional and fight or flight system into gear in 17,000ths of a second, which is at lightning speed. Our emotions can kick into gear faster than any of us can even count.[58]

Our fight or flight system was essential to keeping us alive when we lived amongst the lions and tigers and bears, for obvious reasons. All of our ancestors who did not have such a highly developed fight or flight system, well, they are no longer with us. (This gives truth to the old saying, "I do not have to be faster than the bear. I only have to be faster than you.")

This also explains why we humans are emotional animals, not logical ones. Our fight or flight response is actually designed to be at least twice as fast as our logical brain. Our fight or flight response was designed to keep us alive.[59]

Yes, having a hair-trigger temper probably saved Fred's life several times over. Reacting quickly and distrusting anything that was new to him or looked different from him, including other people, could have easily meant the difference between life and death. He did not have time to reason through his various options when he thought he was being attacked. He had to react quickly, and his brain did just that. It was better to be violent and safe than to be trusting and dead.

Today, our brains react in the exact same way. The truth is that we are all still walking around in the 21st century with a brain that is thousands of years old. Unfortunately, even though our brains have not evolved across the last few thousand years, our world has evolved drastically.[60]

> **We are just cavemen and cavewomen in pants ... but it is time to evolve.**

The Two Human Brains

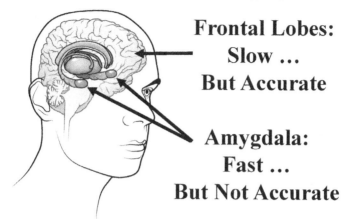

Frontal Lobes: Slow ... But Accurate

Amygdala: Fast ... But Not Accurate

The Amygdala

The amygdala, which looks like two almonds resting on either side of the brain above our ears and behind our eyes, governs our fight or flight response. Our amygdala can trigger our most primal fight or flight response, both consciously and subconsciously, at 17,000ths of a second.[61]

In other words, our amygdala acts like our safety sentinels. They sit behind our eyes and they are always watching to alert us to any kind of perceived danger.

Those same brain functions that served Fred so well 5,000 years ago are now working against us. Today, when we allow Fred's emotional brain and fight or flight system to govern our behavior, we end up getting fired, divorced, and maybe even thrown in jail. Controlling these natural impulses is the basis of emotional intelligence.

The Frontal Lobes

Our frontal lobes control what we commonly call our executive functions, which include our attention span, our ability to focus, to make decisions, to control our fight or flight response, and so on. Our frontal lobes allow us to think and to be logical.

In other words, what our amygdala GENERATES, our frontal lobes REGULATE.

Although you need your frontal lobes to think and to keep your fight or flight response in check, you do not need them to live ... and your body knows that. Whenever Fred Flintstone was attacked on the Serengeti by a lion, to make sure he had the energy he needed to either fight or run away, the blood would instantly rush to the large skeletal muscles in his arms, legs, and lungs. This got him ready for fight or flight. Fighting or running away at that point was more important than making logical decisions.[62]

Unfortunately, this still happens to all of us today. Remember: WE HAVE NOT EVOLVED in the last 5,000 years.

Still today, when our heart rate hits about 145 beats per minute, we all go into full fight or flight. What does that mean? Your body's alarm system will go off and your blood will be automatically re-routed to the large skeletal muscles in your legs, arms, and lungs, preparing your body to either do battle or retreat.[63]

If this distress continues and our heart rate hits about 175 beats per minute, we become what is called "temporarily autistic," according to Dr. Keith Payne, Professor of Psychology and Neuroscience at the University of North Carolina. When this happens to us, we have what feels like an out of body experience. Everything slows down so we can give our undivided attention to whatever is threatening us. Time seems to stand still. Everything becomes surreal.

This reaction protected us whenever a saber-toothed tiger attacked. Its purpose is to focus our attention on nothing else but the tiger.[64]

Now, think about it. If you go into fight or flight, your body automatically reroutes the blood to the large skeletal muscles in your arms, legs, and lungs, just like it did with Fred 5,000 years ago. However, your body did not make any more blood. So ... where did the blood leave?[65]

That's right: Your BRAIN! You are brain impaired![66]

More specifically, the blood just left your frontal lobes. Since your body knows that you do not need your frontal lobes to live, your body treats your frontal lobes like an extra reservoir of blood.[67]

If your frontal lobes lack a proper blood supply, then they will not function properly, which means you lose much of your ability to reason, to make good decisions, and to control your emotions. We then go on automatic and reactive emotional functioning, which is why we revert to our primal instincts so quickly.

Again, how quickly can you jump into a state of fight or flight? Within 17,000ths of a second.

When our frontal lobes lose their blood supply, our emotions overtake our logic because our logical center has largely shut down. The amygdala can easily take control of our behavior because it can trigger our emotions long before the frontal lobes even know what is happening. In other words, when we lose our temper and go into a blind rage, we have been emotionally hijacked. This can happen to us within a fraction of a second because the amygdala can so easily overwhelm the frontal lobes and commandeer the brain.

In this state, people attack each other, they kick their cars, punch walls, and so on. This, at one time or another, happens to all of us.

> **Part of EPR is learning to exercise our frontal lobe's basic functions, which means not letting our amygdala get the better of us.**

The Subconscious Brain

Whenever I am conducting a class on the subconscious or implicit bias, I will ask the attendees if babies cry. They will all answer with a resounding, "Oh, yes!"

I will then ask them if babies laugh. Again, they will all answer, "Yes, of course."

I will then ask them if anyone in the class remembers being born. Of course, no one does. (Thank God for little favors on that one, huh? I mean, there wouldn't be enough therapy in the world to get rid of that mental image.)

So, how can we explain these differences? Why are babies fully alert when they are born, or soon after, reacting to the world around them, yet no one ever remembers any of it?

Well, when we are born, our emotional and our fight or flight systems are pretty much already formed and ready to go. Since our emotional system, or limbic system, is directly wired into our amygdala, that explains why babies are born with the ability to cry, laugh, giggle, and so on. Their emotional and fight or flight systems are primed and ready for action from the very start, just in case there are any saber-toothed tigers still snooping around, or grabby grandparents.

However, our hippocampus, which acts like our short-term memory transmitter, does not fully form until we are about three years old. That is why we don't remember being born, nor do we consciously remember much of anything that happens in our first three years of life.[68]

Why? Because we don't have a functioning hippocampus in our brains to consciously store and transfer this information. No hippocampus ... no cognitive memories. The brain has no way to receive them.

The Powerful Subconscious Brain

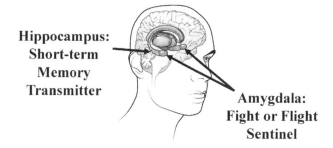

Hippocampus: Short-term Memory Transmitter

Amygdala: Fight or Flight Sentinel

So, if everything we hear, see, feel, taste, and otherwise experience in our first three years of life cannot go into our short-term conscious memory ... where does it go?

RIGHT! Into our emotional and fight or flight systems, which houses part of our subconscious where it will remain forever.

Even though the hippocampus is critical for our short-term conscious memory, our emotional system and the amygdala have independent memory systems of their own. In other words, they do not need the hippocampus to store information into memory and recall it later. Welcome to part of your subconscious.

We all grow up hearing how our friends and relatives speak and how they phrase different words. This information goes into our subconscious where it will remain for the rest of our lives. This is one reason we all naturally have accents without being aware of them. That is how we have been primed.

I always find it amusing when I run into someone who denies the existence of their subconscious mind. They will usually argue that we hear these various accents around us as we grow up, so it goes into our conscious mind.

I will then usually smile and ask them if they have ever curled up in the fetal position and gone to sleep. The person will look at me funny and think about it for a minute. I will then ask them: "Where do you think you got that idea?"

Yes, our subconscious memory system is alive and well even before we are born.

Neuroscience now tells us that our subconscious mind makes up 90% (on the low end) and up to 99% (for people who just never stop and think) of all our thoughts, which includes our decision making.[69] On average, one of the key lessons to understand about the subconscious brain is that it controls about 95% of everything we do all day long. It's really our subconscious beliefs that dictate our behavior and how we see the world.[70]

Most of our subconscious thought processes are purely automatic. They do not need any assistance from our cognitive thoughts to govern our actions. This is why we never think about our accent, driving into work each day, getting ready for work in the morning, or taking our daily pills. We just do it.

We commonly call some of these subconscious acts "habits."

However, we can usually begin to control our subconscious thoughts if we just slow down and think. Unfortunately, few of us ever do that.[71]

To demonstrate how quickly we can all fall victim to our subconscious brain and be primed to react in a certain way, I will often lead my audiences in a little "brainwashing" exercise. I will have my audience say the word "white" along with me ten times quickly. I will then ask them a question and see how long it takes them to answer.

This would actually be a good time for you to play this little game. So, I want you to say the word "white" out loud ten times in a row, then answer the following question:

> ### "What do cows drink?"

OK, how did you do? Cows drink water, right? They don't drink milk, right? Of course, I did not say calves. I did not ask you what baby cows drink.

If you got it wrong, like most people do, you are human. If you are human, your subconscious brain is at least twice as fast as your frontal lobes, and you can be primed, or brainwashed, in just a matter of seconds. Consequently, our subconscious brain can control our conscious mind, and therefore our behavior, without us even knowing it. That is why they call it the "subconscious."

But this is also why, unless your life is truly in danger, your first reaction to a conflict is always wrong. It is wrong because our first reaction always reverts to fight or flight.

I will always tell my audiences that the difference between success and disaster is usually about five seconds. Why? Because it takes about that long for the frontal lobes, our logical brain, to catch up with our amygdala and our emotional brain.

After you said the word "white" ten times, most of you gave the wrong answer to the question you were asked. Why? Because when you just react, you take the low road through your brain, which is a short-cut from your emotional system to your amygdala, and all of this happens at about 17,000ths of a second. That is why most of you answered the question wrong. (Those of you who got it right cheated by thinking for a few seconds before answering, didn't you?)

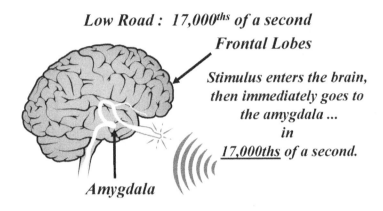

Low Road : 17,000ᵗʰˢ of a second
Frontal Lobes

Stimulus enters the brain,
then immediately goes to
the amygdala ...
in
17,000ths of a second.

Amygdala

However, once you stopped and thought about it for a few precious seconds, you realized you gave the wrong answer because you forced your thought-process to take the high road into your frontal lobes. Since the high road into your conscious brain can take twice as long as our low road through our subconscious, to get the answer right, you have to literally STOP ... think for at least FIVE SECONDS, and THEN give the right answer. Why? Because this gives your frontal lobes a chance to catch up, which enables you to take control over yourself and your thoughts.

That is the first step towards overcoming your subconscious brain.

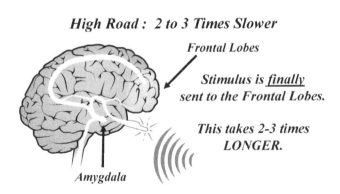

High Road : 2 to 3 Times Slower
Frontal Lobes

Stimulus is finally
sent to the Frontal Lobes.

This takes 2-3 times
LONGER.

Amygdala

To prove this point, I will then give my audiences another word to say, but this time, they will get it right. I will tell them to say the word "top" ten times, and I will ask them another question. However, this time, they will all wait five seconds before they answer. That will give their frontal lobes time to catch up to their subconscious brain and they will get the question right.

Again, this would be a good time for you, the reader, to say the word "top" ten times, then wait five seconds before you answer the next question:

> **"What do you do at a green light?"**

Well? Did you get it right? You go at green lights, right? You don't stop, right?

Yes, the difference between success and failure for the human being in the 21st century can often be as little as five seconds. If we do not first stop to think and let our frontal lobes catch up, the end result can often be disastrous for everyone involved, including you.

Again, we all have accents. But if we slowed down and took that extra five seconds to think about it, many of us could alter our accents. If we practiced it regularly, most of us would begin rewiring our brains and we would soon be able to alter our accents even more. That is also how you start controlling and rewiring your subconscious mind.

These subconscious automatic responses come in very handy for us in our daily lives. Many of us often get dressed in the morning, eat breakfast, drive to work then sit at our desk and think, "How did I get here?" However, when we go into fight or flight, if we humans don't stop and think for a few seconds, we will revert to an evil three-year old version of ourselves, and that will end badly for us.

We all have routines we follow. Humans are definitely creatures of habit and the subconscious brain is the reason why.

Implicit Bias and Confirmation Bias

Whenever we make certain associations in our brains based on someone's race, religion, and so on, we refer to that as bias. [72]

Implicit bias (or subconscious bias) refers to the stereotypes, opinions, and attitudes that live in our subconscious brain, all of which directly influence the way we view the world, the way we interpret what others say, and the decisions we all make ... all in a subconscious way. For our purposes, whenever I refer to someone's implicit bias, I am simply referring to how someone has subconsciously categorized other people in their mind.

Confirmation bias (or cognitive bias), on the other hand, is the human tendency to only seek out and accept information that confirms what we already believe to be true. We humans tend to discount and rationalize away any opinions or facts that contradict our existing point of view. In other words ...

> **Confirmation bias puts into action the implicit bias living in all of us.**

Confirmation bias is also why humans interpret any ambiguous evidence, evidence that does not support one side or the other, as supporting their existing position. Thanks to confirmation bias, the facts only get in the way of a good opinion. We rush to judgment and often make bad decisions based on faulty information.

Sometimes, we use confirmation bias in a very conscious way to justify what we are already doing. Even though we often call this explicit bias, it has its roots in the subconscious.

Implicit and confirmation bias are vital topics to grasp if you are truly going to understand how humans think and make decisions.

Whenever you see someone actively engaging in some form of hate speech, I assure you, they believe what they are saying. However, according to Dr. Bruce Lipton, the roots of these beliefs come from their subconscious, which typically controls about 95% of what we do all day long, and that includes our overt acts. So, attacking the true source of our beliefs, which rests in our subconscious brain, is the key.

We humans do this in our everyday lives ... and politicians have made a career of it. We try to make something sound better by distorting the truth with a euphemism.[73] For instance:

- "I bought a Pre-Certified Car," which really means, "I bought a used car."
- "Janet had a wardrobe malfunction," which really means, "Janet just flashed everyone."
- "We lost dad," which really means, "Dad died."
- "We suffered some collateral damage," which really means "Oops! We killed some people by mistake."
- "He was killed by friendly fire," which really means, "Oops! We shot our own guy."
- "Senator Bob relayed misinformation," which really means, "Senator Bob lied."

Such euphemisms are just another way to misdirect others or ourselves, and we usually like it. It makes us feel better about dealing with something that is bad.

Priming & Projection

How We View The World

Priming IN ...

(Implicit Bias)

Projection OUT ...

(Confirmation Bias)

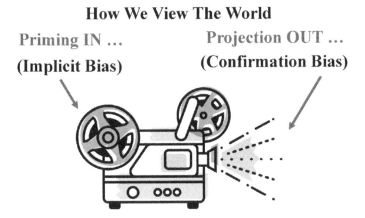

Understanding the subconscious effects of implicit and confirmation bias makes it much easier to understand the principles of priming and projection, which we all live with every day of our lives.

- We are all products of our environments. That means we have all been primed to view the world in a certain way from our various experiences. This priming affects how we see the world, which is called projection.

- Therefore, projection brings action and life to our priming.

It is probably best to think of priming and projection like having a movie projector in our heads. How we prime this projector is up to us and the people around us. Whatever movie you prime into the projector is the movie you will see. If you prime a Mister Rogers movie into this projector, then you will project and see wonderful things everywhere. However, if you prime in *The Godfather* movie, then you will pretty much see murders and dead bodies everywhere. The environment that you expose your brain to will determine what categories you will create in your brain and how you will label other people.

And don't forget: We are all human beings, which means we are all wired to prime our subconscious projectors from *before* we were even born. It is a universal trait among humans.[74] It also explains why what you say about other people tells me a whole lot more about you than it does about the other person.

There is an old saying that beautifully reflects this phenomenon of projection:

> **When the pickpocket sees the Saint, all the pickpocket sees are the Saint's pockets.**

Priming & Influencing Behavior

John Bargh is a psychologist who formed the ACME (or Automaticity in Cognition, Motivation, and Emotion) Lab at Yale University. ACME, an organization that focuses on the affects the subconscious has on our psychological and behavioral processes, has developed a way to measure the effect our subconscious has on our behavior. It is called the "Priming Experiment."[75]

In one experiment, Bargh administered a test to two groups of 60 New York University students, with 30 students in each group. Each group was given different sentences to unscramble. However, there were two versions of these scrambled sentences:[76]

One group of sentences contained words primed to relate to elderly stereotypes, such as worried, Florida, retired, bitter, old, lonely, gray, selfishly, bingo, and wrinkle, to mention a few. However, the other list of sentences that needed to be unscrambled contained only neutral words.[77]

Each participant took their tests one at a time and were told to unscramble the sentences they were given. After the participant completed the task and notified the instructor, the instructor ended the exercise. The instructor then told the participant that the elevator was down the hall and thanked him or her for participating.[78]

However, sitting outside the testing room was a "confederate" who had a hidden stopwatch and recorded how long it took each participant to walk the length of the hallway.[79]

In two separate test groups, the results were the same:

> The group of students who were given the additional words that primed them to think "old" took much longer to walk down the hall than did the other group.[80]

According to Bargh, the important message of these experiments is that humans can be automatically and subconsciously programmed to change their behavior based on the stereotypes we all carry with us.[81]

So, what should you do to avoid the subconscious effects of priming? According to Bargh, you simply become more mindful of what is happening. You slow down and think!

Bargh says that he could imagine situations where the consequences of exhibiting bad behavior would be detrimental to your well-being, such as when you are talking to your boss. In that situation, even if you have been primed to be angry or frustrated, you would most likely cool your heels a little better if you were talking with your boss.[82]

In other words, you probably would do a much better job taking those vital five seconds to slow down and let your frontal lobes catch up.

The Ohio State University's Kirwan Institute

Cheryl Staats of The Ohio State University's Kirwan Institute authored the *State of the Science: Implicit Bias Review*, which brings together a broad range of research on how unconscious racial associations influence human decision-making and outcomes. Staat *t Bias Review* highlights how our subconscious brain shapes our behavior without us even knowing it.[83]

With the controversy surrounding the deadly altercation between George Zimmerman and Trayvon Martin, Staats and the Kirwan Institute saw the opportunity to research how implicit bias may have played a role between Martin and Zimmerman, as well as during Zimmerman's trial.

If you briefly recall, Trayvon Martin was a 17-year-old Black male who was shot to death by George Zimmerman, a neighborhood watch volunteer, in Sanford, Florida on the evening of February 26, 2013.

That evening, Martin was walking to his father's house. He walked through a neighborhood where several robberies had recently occurred. Zimmerman, who volunteered to be on the neighborhood watch that night, saw Martin out walking. Zimmerman called the Sanford Police to report Martin's suspicious behavior. A few minutes later, a fight broke out between the two. Zimmerman then shot Martin in the chest.

Apparently, Martin punched Zimmerman when Zimmerman stopped him. As a result, Zimmerman was not originally charged for shooting Martin by the Sanford Police, claiming that Zimmerman was defending himself under Florida's Stand Your Ground Law. The police claimed that the law prohibited them from arresting or charging Zimmerman because they did not have any clear evidence to refute his defense.

However, after this tragedy got national attention, Zimmerman was eventually charged and tried in Martin's death. Zimmerman was acquitted of second-degree murder and manslaughter in July 2013.

After George Zimmerman was acquitted for killing Trayvon Martin, the interest in implicit and confirmation bias skyrocketed. After analyzing volumes of research, Staats concluded:

> **Implicit bias overwhelmingly influences how both White and Black Americans alike view Blacks as being more violent and dangerous than other groups.**

In one study, researchers subliminally primed participants with either a Black male face, a White male face, or no face at all. The participants were then shown degraded images that slowly became clearer to the participants. Some of the objects shown to the participants were related to violence, such as a photo of a gun or a knife, while others were more innocent items, such as a camera or a pocket watch.[84]

Participants were told to identify the exact moment when they could distinguish what the object was coming into focus. The findings showed when the participants had been primed by seeing a Black face first, they identified the crime-related objects much faster. Again, this was true of all the participants regardless of their race.[85]

On the night that George Zimmerman killed Trayvon Martin, he had a gun with him. Clearly, this fact could have had a great influence on how Zimmerman saw Trayvon that night. So, the question then becomes, "Would Zimmerman's perception be influenced by the fact that he was holding a gun?" The research suggests he would.

In five experiments conducted by psychology professors at the University of Notre Dame and Purdue University, participants were given a toy gun or a foam ball to hold. They were then flashed pictures of different people across a computer screen holding either a toy gun, a cell phone, or something else. Regardless of what picture the participants were shown, the participants holding the toy guns were more likely to say that the people on the screen were also holding a gun, even when they were not.[86]

In short, whatever you are primed to think about ... that is what you will tend to see.

Law professor Justin Levinson researched implicit bias and how it might influence the way jurors recall the facts from a case. Participants served as mock jurors and were divided into three groups. All three groups were given the exact same story to read about a fistfight. However, in each of these three groups, the main character in the story changed. One group read about William, a Caucasian man, another group read about Tyronne, an African American man, and the final group read about Kawika, a Hawaiian man.

When the jurors were later asked to recall the details of the fight, Levinson found that the mock jurors were significantly more likely to recall the aggressive facts from the story when Tyronne was the main character, as opposed to those who read about this same fight but it involved either a Caucasian or a Hawaiian man.[87]

Levinson found that the greatest factor that affected the jurors' ability to recall the facts of the story was their own implicit bias *based on the race of the accused.*

So, can taking the time to slow down and think really overcome something as strong as our subconscious or implicit biases? Absolutely.

One study considered the group decision-making processes used by mock juries.

The study found that the more racially diverse juries deliberated longer and considered a wider range of facts before reaching their final verdict than did the all-White juries, which should in and of itself be a good justification for diversity. Actually, the more racially diverse juries took a much harder look at whether the issue of race was playing a role in their decisions. The researchers found that implicit bias, like all stereotypes, myths, and stigmas, tend to die when exposed to the light.[88]

Research on implicit bias shows that jurors actually show less bias when a case is more racially charged. This is because in racially charged cases, jurors are more aware of the role race plays in the case. As with most anything, the more prevalent the issue of race is in a case, the more the jury will be aware of it. This awareness forces them to slow down their thought processes and consider if race truly is a factor, which helps to eliminate its subconscious effects in deliberations.[89]

Unfortunately, the jury in the Zimmerman trial never even discussed the issue of race.

For instance, when Juror B37 was interviewed by Anderson Cooper, she said that the jurors did not even consider that race might be a factor in making their decision. This juror actually said, "I think all of us thought race did not play a role. We never had that discussion."[90]

Therefore, by putting the issue of race on the back burner and not explicitly addressing it, implicit bias was even more likely to influence the jurors' opinions subconsciously. Again, research clearly shows that implicit bias proliferates most when it is ignored.

So, what does all this mean?

> **People ... are people ... are people, and we are all cursed with the same brain structure.**

Whenever we see someone we do not know, we all reach into our subconscious bag of stereotypes, or our MSU File (or Make Stuff Up), and label that other person in 17,000ths of a second.

I think of implicit and confirmation bias every day of my life and I work hard to make sure I do not fall prey to it. Whenever I am in the office working on trivial things, I have my TV set turned to CNN. I will then turn it over to Fox News. I will then turn it to MSNBC. I will then switch to another source of information.

Why?

Because everyone and everything has their own slants and biases and when I form my opinions, I want to know what each side is saying about the issues. I don't want to be a bullying, intolerant, bigoted, emotional child.

Today's research supports this way of overcoming these biases and prejudices. But again, we humans rarely do that, but we need to start, five seconds at a time.

The Darker Side of Our Subconscious

Unfortunately, in the worst of all possible scenarios, our sub-conscious plays tricks with how we perceive the world with disastrous ends. Consider the horrendous case of Amadou Diallo.

Amadou was born in Liberia on September 2, 1975. He came from an affluent family and lived in what some would call a mansion. He went to private schools where he studied English and computer engineering in Singapore and Thailand.[91]

Amadou immigrated to America in 1996 to pursue his dream of getting a college education and to experience the United States. When he left for America, his mother asked him if he needed anything. He told her, "Just your prayers." He wanted to make it on his own.[92]

People who knew Amadou described him as a shy, hard-working man who was always ready with a smile. He was a devout Muslim who did not drink and prayed five times a day, even if he had to do it in a crowded room. Friends said Amadou would often reach into his pocket and give money to the beggars he saw on the street. He would also lend money to students who went to the high school near him. For instance, Amadou lent Mohammed Ahmed, a 20-year-old student, $43.00 so he could pay his income taxes. That is what it was like to have Amadou Diallo in your life.[93]

Five days before he was killed, Amadou called his mother. He told her he loved her and that he had raised $9,000.00 to pay for college. He was making his living by selling video cassettes, gloves, and socks on the sidewalk during the day in Manhattan, often working twelve-hour days and not getting back home until after midnight. Although he was struggling, Amadou was making it on his own and he was on his way to reaching his dream of going to college and becoming a computer programmer. That was the last conversation he would ever have with his mother.[94]

At about 12:40 am on February 4, 1999, Amadou was standing near the entrance of his doorway after getting home from a late dinner. He was smoking a cigarette to relax. At that same time, four plain-clothed New York City police officers, Edward McMellon, age 26, Sean Carroll, age 35, Kenneth Boss, age 26, and Richard Murphy, age 26, slowly drove by Diallo's doorway.[95]

The four officers were part of the elite plain clothed Street Crimes Unit, which has been described as an aggressive unit that largely focused on taking illegal guns off the street. Due to the nature of their work, that is how they were trained. That was what they knew.[96]

The Street Crimes Unit's motto was, "We own the night." They had t-shirts printed with a quote from Ernest Hemingway's book, *On the Blue Water:* "Certainly there is no hunting like the hunting of a man."[97]

The officers carried 9-millimeter semiautomatic pistols, which hold 16 bullets. These officers could empty their entire clip in seconds.[98]

All four of the plainclothes officers also wore bulletproof vests, which made them look huge to Diallo, who was only about five foot six inches tall and weighed 150 pounds.[99]

Carroll was the first to spot Diallo standing out in front of the building. Carroll told Boss, "Hold up, hold up. What's that guy doing there?"

The officers later testified that it never occurred to any of them that maybe Amadou actually lived in the building.[100]

As the car slowed down, stopped and then backed up, Amadou apparently became concerned. He peeked in and out of the shadows in front of his doorway.[101]

Carroll and McMellon got out of the car. "Police," McMellon called out, holding up his badge. "Can we have a word?"

Amadou didn't answer. Again, English was at best Amadou's second language. This fact, coupled with the rush of fear he certainly felt as these large White men dressed in civilian clothes were coming towards him holding guns, makes it easy to conclude that Amadou probably did not understand what they were saying. The adrenaline rush most of us would experience would make our ability to process information shut down.[102]

What the police did not know is that Amadou had a stutter, so he might have tried to say something back, but couldn't.[103]

Amadou also knew someone who was recently robbed by a group of armed men in the neighborhood. This only added to the probability that Amadou was truly afraid of the large armed men coming towards him. Also, this is the south Bronx. It is not a nice neighborhood and it was well after midnight.

Seeing this happening in front of him, Amadou froze for a second, then ran into the vestibule of his apartment building. Carroll and McMellon ran after him with their guns drawn and yelling.

Amadou only got as far as the inside door of his vestibule, which was locked. He was trapped. He frantically grabbed the doorknob with his left hand, turned his body to the side and kept digging into his pockets with his right hand.

Carroll yelled at Amadou, "Show me your hands!"

McMellon yelled out, "Get your hands out of your pockets. Don't make me kill you!"

However, Amadou only became more frantic. He then reached into his back pocket and started to remove something.

At that point, Carroll yelled out, "Gun! He's got a gun!" He then fired his weapon.

Two of the officers, Carroll and McMellon, emptied their weapons, firing 16 shots each. Boss fired his gun five times and Murphy fired four times. This was a total of 41 shots fired by the officers, hitting Diallo 19 times.[104]

Amadou was dead.

What the officers saw was not a gun. It was a wallet.[105]

Not only did the officers fire 41 shots, but they only hit Amadou 19 times from a pretty close range. This shows how frantic the police officers themselves were that night.

But they are the police. Isn't their job to control these types of situations, especially since they initiated the first contact with Amadou? Wasn't it their job to not escalate the situation and to keep emotions, like fear, from getting out of hand? Yelling at someone and giving them orders in the middle of the night is probably not the best way to do that. It is dangerous for the public and it is dangerous for the police officers. So, why did they approach the situation like this?

Because that is how they were trained. This elite unit was not trained to de-escalate and control situations. This unit was trained to be aggressive, to be violent. The training they received doomed Amadou and all four of these police officers.

What I would want to know is what the heart rates of these officers were when they opened fire? Remember, when our heart rate hits 145 beats per minute, our body will go into full fight or flight. However, when our heart rate hits 175 beats per minute, we become temporarily autistic. This means everything will slow way down for us and we tend to have an out of body experience. Our brain will go largely on automatic and rely on our instincts, which includes our subconscious and the training we have been given.[106]

We will rely on the way we have been programmed or primed.

This also explains why these officers fired so many shots at Amadou. After he had been hit the first couple of times, that was enough. He was not going to be able to resist anymore. Still, the spray of bullets continued in such an uncontrolled way that these officers even shot Amadou while he was lying prostrate on the ground. One bullet went through the bottom of his foot and exited through the top. Another bullet entered his calf just above the right ankle and lodged in the back of his knee. The only way to explain the trajectory of both of these wounds is that he was shot when he was lying prone on the ground.[107]

This total loss of control by these police officers also explains why they saw a gun in Amadou's hand when it was just a wallet. All their training had primed them to see a gun.

This entire situation was initiated by the police, it was escalated by the police, and it ended in a hail of bullets fired by the police.

Why? Because these police officers are human beings, just like you and me, and this is exactly what they were trained, or primed, to do. If you ever hear that we have a "Systematic Police" problem, this is a big part of it right here. This must change for the sake of the public and the police officers themselves.

"The Police Officer's Dilemma"

After Amadou Diallo was killed, psychologists Joshua Correll, Charles Judd, Bernadette Park, and Bernd Wittenbrink conducted a research study to examine the effects one's ethnicity has on humans in shoot or don't shoot situations.

Using a simple video game, various people, who we will call targets, were shown to the participants as they played the game. The targets who flashed across the screen were either holding a gun, an aluminum can, a wallet, or a cell phone. The participants were then told to shoot the targets who were armed and to not shoot the targets who were unarmed.[108]

This situation is known as the "Police Officer's Dilemma."[109]

However, the participants were not told that some of the targets were White and some were Black. Over the course of four studies, researchers found what they called "shooter bias." This means the participants were faster to correctly shoot an armed suspect if he was Black and to correctly not shoot an unarmed suspect if he was White.[110]

However, the alarming and sad discovery was that:

> **All of the participants were consistently more likely to shoot an unarmed suspect if he was Black regardless of the race of the participant.**

Of course, who does not realize there are more prejudicial stereotypes against Blacks in American society than Whites? If you doubt this at all, let's say you were driving along in your car and were pulled over and questioned by a police officer. At the exact second you were pulled over, let's say you could choose the color of your skin. What color would you choose?

The Fatal Cost to the Police

Yes, the police have an impossible job to do. However, their job is made even harder, if not impossible, by the training they often receive.

I was once told by an HR person with a suburban police department that she liked my Five Skills of Tolerance program, but there was just too much brain stuff.

Hearing such responses just makes me sad. You cannot understand how implicit bias works, and then how to rewire yourself, if you do not understand why your brain works the way it does. Unfortunately, that is one reason so many police departments across this country have failed to effectively help their officers deal with and correct the critical issue of implicit bias.

In all fairness to the law enforcement agencies who have really tried to address these issues and have spent millions of dollars trying to train their officers properly, this is the type of advice they usually get from the diversity experts. It is often the same type of rhetoric that I have heard for the last 20 years at various D&I conferences across this country, much of which I have already described to you.

As the old saying goes:

> **"Ignorance" is not knowing something.**
> **"Stupidity" is doing the same thing again and again and expecting a different result.**

Again, there are great diversity people out there who do understand these concepts, However, that is clearly not the norm.

CBS News did a remarkable study on how so many police departments across this country have instituted implicit bias training since Trayvon Martin was killed. However, according to this report, only about 69% of the police departments across this country have instituted some sort of implicit bias training. That means about one-third of all the law enforcement agencies across this country have done nothing to address this issue of implicit bias ... and they just might be the smart ones.[112]

Think about it. If 69% of the police departments across this country have instituted real implicit bias training, then why are we still seeing so many of the George Floyd, Elijah McClain, and Walter Scott type of killings these days?

According to the CBS News report, officers claimed the implicit bias session they were given was the worst training they have ever received. Even after they took the training, many officers still claimed that they did not see the value of the program because they did not see that they might have a problem. They did not believe that their subconscious could possibly be interfering with their perception or that they suffered from any implicit bias at all, even though they are all human.[113]

Of course, like every other group of people on the planet, there are bad cops. You have already met many of them on the evening news. Yes, some officers need to lose their badges, just as some lawyers need to be disbarred. Remember: No one hates the bad employees as much as the good ones, and that goes for cops as well.

Even more disturbing, not only was the training not effective in changing the attendees' attitudes towards implicit bias, but much of the time was spent telling White police officers they are racists. This is simply not how you win anyone over and get them to change how they think, but that is what too many D&I programs do. This must stop.[114]

Also, it is impossible to ignore the personal toll the lack of proper training takes on these officers as individual human beings.

Constantly going into fight or flight will flood your brain with adrenaline and cortisol, which will eventually damage it. It is this type of flooding that has given so many of our police officers crippling mental conditions, such as PTSD, which can make them even more predisposed to violent or aberrant behavior.[115]

When I say such training is vital not just for the public's sake but for the police officers as well, I am dead serious. About one-third of all active and retired police officers suffer from PTSD, and most don't even realize it. It is also estimated 150,000 police officers have suffered from PTSD. Consequently, more police officers die by suicide than are killed in the line of duty.[116]

According to the NAMI, or the National Alliance on Mental Health, nearly 1 in 4 police officers have thoughts of suicide at some point in their lives. Even in the smallest police departments, the suicide rate of officers is still four times the national average compared to the general population.[117]

It is time for us to learn D&I in a whole new way.

Rewiring Our Brains: Educating Our Subconscious

STEP ONE:
Discover What Is in Your Subconscious.

Before you can become more mindful of your actions and your thoughts, you must first become more self-aware and discover what is truly living in your subconscious. You must identify your own biases and prejudices, your strengths and weaknesses, and your trigger points in order to address them.

To discover the degree of bigotry that lives in our subconscious, psychologists devised the Implicit Association Test (or the IAT). The IAT is designed to measure associations we don't even know we have because they live deep within our subconscious brain.[118]

The IAT is an assessment tool that quantifies the degree of implicit bias we all hold in our subconscious brain. The IAT measures the subconscious associations we all have but don't know are there.[119]

The IAT is a computer program that requires the user to choose between two different targets, like between a White person and a Black person, or a male and a female, and so on. The faster responses are interpreted as favoring the image of the target shown to them, while slower responses by the user are viewed as being unfavorable to the user. The users must make split second decisions in reacting to these target images. Researchers claim that our IAT scores reflect either our subconscious beliefs or the true attitudes people have but are not willing to share publicly.[120]

A typical IAT assessment has the user complete several tasks. In short, the IAT measures your reaction time to different types of people. For this discussion, however, we will look at the IAT based upon race.[121]

At the beginning of the test, you are asked about your attitudes regarding Blacks and Whites. Most people say that they believe both races of people are equal. The researchers then show you a Black face, then a White face, then a Black face, and so on. You are then asked to judge whether the face is friendly or unfriendly. Since the test measures your reaction time in fractions of a second, whether you have a bias in favor of White people or a prejudice against people of color, it can be measured in milliseconds. Since you are never sure what color the face will be that appears next, your subconscious plays a major role in how quickly you react, or more importantly, if you react incorrectly to the face that appears.

If you react more slowly to a friendly Black face, the test concludes that you have a prejudice against Black people, and the test quantifies your score.

If you would like to test your own level of bias and prejudice in many different areas, you can use Harvard University's Individual Assessment Technique, or IAT. I have set up a hotlink on my website at www.scottwarrick.com under the *Living The Five Skills of Tolerance* icon that will take you right to this free assessment. Several tests are there for you to take, including the Race IAT, as we just discussed.

You cannot begin to rewire your subconscious brain until you know what is in there first. Few people will try to improve on something if they do not realize there is a problem. Taking this test will certainly do that for you. That is why whenever I conduct a seminar on implicit bias or my Five Skills of Tolerance, I always have the attendees take the IAT test before they even arrive at the session. Actually, most people are ashamed of their scores, thinking they are bad racist people. Many will freely admit that they were shocked by their scores. It also sets the stage for some great in-class discussion, which often goes back to that person's childhood priming.

Having said that, just because you have an implicit bias does not make you a racist. It means you are a human, and as a human, you have a choice in how you confront and address your biases and prejudices.

Coming to the seminar prepared ahead of time helps to show the attendees that we have some work to do. It proves to everyone that there are indeed termites living in their subconscious, and they need to get rid of them. This is a wonderful, and free, needs assessment.

After that, most people can't wait to learn more about their brain and how to rewire it.

Of course, once you discover what biases live in your subconscious brain, the next question to ask is, "OK, I now see where I have some underlying prejudices. What do I do about it?"

STEP TWO:
Slow Down and Think ... and Use Your EPR Skills!

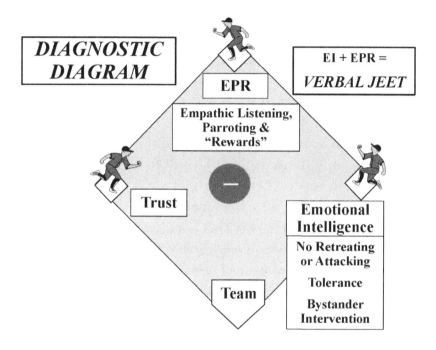

By now, you had to see this coming.

This is how you start becoming more mindful: Slow down and think before you engage your mouth. Otherwise, you think you should stop at green lights or that cows drink milk.

Remember: The difference between success and failure is often just five seconds.

In my book, *Solve Employee Problems Before They Start: Resolving Conflict in the Real World,* I focused my attention on first and second base, as you will see in the previous diagram. To properly address any conflict, you have to first slow down and let your frontal lobes catch up with your emotional system so you can remain in control of your ego and emotions. That is emotional intelligence. That is first base.

Once you can control yourself, then you can move onto second base, which is using your EPR Skills to resolve conflict. Again, EPR stands for Empathic Listening, Parroting, and "Rewards." That is why I published my other book first: It describes in great detail what emotional intelligence really is and how you can start to establish it as part of your own life, and then how you can use your EPR skills to better address and resolve conflict. Both of these skills are critical to mastering the Five Skills of Tolerance.

When you sequentially combine emotional intelligence with your ability to use your EPR skills to address and resolve a conflict, that is what I call "Verbal Jeet."

I often am asked why I tie martial arts to the subject of emotional intelligence. In my first book, *Solve Employee Problems Before They Start: Resolving Conflict in the Real World*, I explained that it is a throwback to Bruce Lee's simplified version of Kung Fu, which he called Jeet Kune Do.

Another reason is because studying martial arts has been shown to increase one's level of emotional intelligence. In 2014, Dr. Daniel Baczkowski, Dr. Cheri Hampton-Farmer, Dr. Chris Moser and Matthew Moser of the University of Findlay published their abstract, *Emotional Intelligence in the Martial Arts: Predictor of Success* in the *Journal of Scholastic Inquiry: Behavioral Sciences*. Their research showed that individuals who had earned at least a first-degree black belt had higher scores on their BarOn EQ-i assessments than those found in the general population. Why is that? Dr. Moser claims that in martial arts, there are "specific values, or tenets" that all of its students are required to follow. In short, learning martial arts teaches its pupils how to gain more control over their egos and emotions, which allows them to better address and resolve conflicts. Just as everyone who studies martial arts is expected to follow those principles, every employee should also be required to follow the organization's core values, which must include the Five Skills of Tolerance, including the skills of EPR.

So, how do you define "respect"? EPR. If someone is not starting the conflict discussion by using their Empathic Listening Skills, then Parroting everything back to the other person to the other person's satisfaction, and then giving that other person a "Reward" whenever they disagree (i.e. "I understand what you are telling me, but what about this ..."), then the chances the two parties will resolve the conflict are greatly reduced.

That is why I love the EPR system and cannot go a single day without it. Those are the only three moves you will ever need to resolve a conflict. It is simple enough for anyone to use ... if they choose to do so.

The first step in resolving any conflict with our EPR system is Empathic Listening. This is vintage Stephen Covey: "Seek first to understand, then seek to be understood." In other words, you need to shut up and just listen!

Starting a conflict discussion is easy. You begin with your Empathic Listening, which means you would say something like, "Look, this has been bothering me, so I wanted to touch base with you and hear your side. I want to understand where you are coming from because I want to resolve this and make sure that you and I are good."

And then, you shut up and focus on what the other person is saying from their perspective. That is Empathic Listening, and it takes tremendous focus. Empathic Listening not only forces you to slow down and think, but it lets you hear where the other person is coming from. If you are a 60-year-old White guy trying to resolve a conflict with a 22-year-old Black female, do you think you see the world the same? Of course not.

Parroting is the next step, and Parroting keeps your Empathic Listening honest. Parroting back to the other person what they just said to their satisfaction ensures that you really have engaged in Empathic Listening. This ensures there is a real common understanding between you and the other person.

To Parrot something back to the other person, you simply say something like, "OK, now let me make sure I've got this. You are telling me this ... and this ... and that. Do I understand?"

If the other person disagrees, then you clearly misunderstood something. So, you go back and listen again. You do not move on in the conversation until the other person agrees that you really did restate their position to their satisfaction. It ensures a common understanding with the other person.

Once you have Parroted everything back to the other person's satisfaction, great. You can move on in the discussion.

That brings you to the final step in the EPR process, which is giving the other person a "Reward." You only give someone a "Reward" when you are going to disagree with them. You never have to give someone a "Reward" if you agree. The agreement is compliment enough. People, after all, rarely get angry with you when you agree with them.

For instance, let's say the other person actually tells you something you didn't know, so you change your mind. You agree with the other person. The other person will be thrilled. (Well, maybe not thrilled, but you get the idea.)

However, the danger comes when the other person has not changed your mind and you still disagree with them. Whenever you disagree with another human, you have to give them a "Reward."

It is important to realize that humans marry their opinions. Our opinions on highly emotional matters are tied directly to our self-esteem. Whenever I disagree with someone and say something like, "Where did you get that idea?" or "That is the dumbest thing I ever heard," or "I disagree. You're wrong," I just called the other person stupid.

Did you just feel your gut twinge a little bit when you read my responses? That was you going into a little bit of fight or flight mode because I just insulted you. I didn't mean to call you stupid, but by demeaning your opinion like that, I just did. In other words: I just showed you that it was not safe to disagree with me. I harmed the trust between us.

I was intolerant of your opinion, and that violates our relationship and culture.

Instead, whenever I disagree with you, I need to give you a "Reward." This means that even though I am disagreeing with you, I will also validate your right to have an opinion different from mine.

Giving someone a "Reward" means you are trying to protect their self-esteem and show them they have a right to their own opinion, but you simply disagree with them on this particular topic. Remember: You are dealing with a human, the most emotional and most dangerous animal on the planet. That human can turn on you in 17,000ths of a second.

So, in order to give me a "Reward," you would say something like, "I see what you are saying, but I also think ..." or "I understand where you are coming from, but what about this ..." and so on.

The key to addressing and resolving conflict lies in gaining control over your ego and emotions, which is emotional intelligence, and using your EPR skills.

Of course, once you have controlled yourself, and then used your EPR skills to address the conflict, you have now shown the other person that it is safe to disagree with you. That takes you to third base, which is trust.

For more information on building and using your EPR skills, just go to my website at www.scottwarrick.com and click onto the *Living The Five Skills of Tolerance* icon.

STEP THREE:
REWIRE Your Subconscious by Seeking out People Who Are Different from You

Yes, you can physically rewire your subconscious brain. Today, neuroscience shows us how to do this.

Neuroscientists today refer to our brains as being plastic, which means our brain will actually reshape itself, or rewire itself, with every social interaction we experience to become more efficient, more effective, and to adapt to its environment. Scientists refer to this phenomenon as neuroplasticity.[122]

Neuroplasticity, or the reshaping of our current neurons, occurs whenever our brain cells fire and messages are transmitted between them.

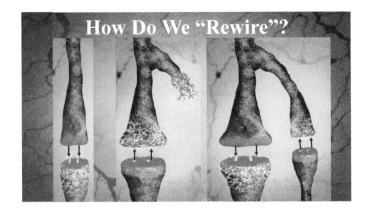

In the previous diagram, you will see three neurons. The neuron on the far left is a single brain cell firing. However, as this neuron fires again and again and again, it will actually receive more firings or activity than it can handle. So, it will go into overload. To handle all of the activity it is receiving, this neuron will grow a new extension or sprout, as you can see in the middle diagram.

In the far-right neuron, you can see that the original neuron has grown an entirely new sprout so it can better transmit the messages being sent into this area of the brain.

This is how you rewire your brain, including your subconscious.

This is also why concert violinists and pianists have so many more synapses in the hand and finger coordination areas of their brains than the rest of us. They have practiced their craft so many times that they have actually rewired their brains and added millions of new neurons to the region of their brains that control hand and finger coordination.[123]

What we have learned about neuroplasticity has given birth to the field of social epigenetics. Social epigenetics is the study of how the neurons in our brains change in response to the outside world. The cells in our brains physically change in response to our everyday experiences.

This is why so many of you have always heard that it takes about 30 days of doing something to form a habit. That is correct because it takes most people about that long to practice something enough to rewire that portion of their brain.

For instance, suppose you were transferred to a new work location. For the first few weeks, you would really have to focus on what you were doing because you would not be used to driving that route. However, after a while, you would get more and more used to it. Eventually, you would not have to think about it at all. You could just about put your brain on cruise control and it could automatically get you to work without you even thinking about it.

Further, besides reshaping the neurons that already exist in our brains, we also grow brand new neurons every month. We used to think that humans were born with all the neurons and synapses they would ever possess, but that is not true. We now know that the brain and spinal cord contain stem cells that grow into thousands of new neurons every day. We humans can actually grow 100,000 new neurons each month, with each of these new brain cells also growing additional sprouts.[124]

Another way to think about forming new neural pathways in our brains is to think of a fresh blanket of snow on the ground. At first, you cannot see the street or the sidewalk. But when the first person walks through the snow and onto the sidewalk, a slight path is formed. If no other people follow this trail, then it will simply blow away and disappear. However, as more people follow the footsteps laid down by the first person who walked through the snow, the path becomes more pronounced. It becomes stronger and stronger until eventually it becomes a vivid pathway that is easy to follow.[125]

That is how the circuitry in our brain works to form habits and to develop skills. The first neural circuitry connections we make initially are weak. However, as we repeat the process again and again and again, the neural circuits become stronger every time we repeat the thought process until eventually these neural pathways become so strong that our behavior becomes automatic. We then instinctively follow this new neural circuit.

Thomas Pettigrew is a social psychologist who has studied prejudice for over three decades. Over this period of time, Pettigrew has overseen one of the world's largest databases of studies focusing on why our prejudicial views of other people change when we have contact with those people we don't like. Pettigrew and his associates analyzed over 515 studies dating from the 1940's to 2000. They combined this data into one massive statistical analysis. The responses came from all across the planet: 250,493 people from thirty-eight countries. The Us v. Them prejudices included all kinds of ethnic, racial, and religious prejudices from all over the world, including the Black-White relations in the United States.[126]

Pettigrew's conclusion:

> **When we have emotional involvements with those people we look down on and consider inferior, those attachments make us far more accepting of each other's differences.[127]**

Pettigrew also concluded:

> **The essential requirement for overcoming prejudice is getting a strong emotional connection with the target group.[128]**

Let's say you just took an IAT assessment and you were unhappy with your score. What do you do about it?

In one study, people who held implicit prejudices against Blacks were shown photos of widely admired Black celebrities, such as Oprah, President Obama, Martin Luther King, Jr., and of course, the great American-Muslim philosopher, Dave Chappelle. They were then shown photographs of White people who were widely despised, such as serial killer Jeffrey

Dahmer. The subjects were shown a total of only forty photographs, so their exposure to these subjects was minimal ... just one fifteen-minute session.[129]

However, that brief fifteen-minute tutorial was enough to rewire these subjects' subconscious. As a result, the IAT scores of these subjects improved dramatically. Subconscious anti-Black attitudes vanished. Twenty-four hours later, their IAT scores remained high.[130]

Why does this exposure to positive Black role models work? Because you are *rewiring* your brain ... literally. Again, it is so obvious that it evades us. We literally rewire our brains a little bit with each thought or action we perform, which is exactly what we all do when we form a new habit.

This neurological phenomenon is what Mahzarin Banaji of Harvard University was describing when she said, "I had a student who used to take the IAT every day. It was the first thing he did, and his idea was just to let the data gather as he went. Then this one day, he got a positive association with Blacks. And he said, 'That's odd. I've never gotten that before,' because we've all tried to change our IAT score and we couldn't. But he's a track-and-field guy, and what he realized is that he'd spent the morning watching the Olympics." This increased exposure to positive Black role models had made the difference. It changed the way the student viewed Black people. It had changed the way he really thought in his subconscious, which directly altered his explicit actions.[131]

That is the key to rewiring your subconscious brain. According to Dr. Lipton, the minute you change your perception is the moment you rewrite the chemistry of your body.[132]

This is how you cure the human disease of being a bullying, intolerant, bigoted, emotional child.

My Personal Project

Whenever I have a bad encounter with someone who is a minority, I use the principles I teach in this book to rewire my brain. I go to my own Personal Project Plan.

I always have my own Personal Project Plan ready to go whenever I find myself in bad or confrontational situations. My Personal Project Plan reminds me of what I can do whenever I have bad experiences about anything.

I have documentaries and movies that I can watch on various types of minorities that portray them in a positive light, rather than those based on myths or stereotypes. This is really easy to do today with all the streaming services available out there. Actually, today, I have a whole list of movies I recommend to my clients whom I am coaching. You will find a listing of these various movies on my website at www.scottwarrick.com under the *Living The Five Skills of Tolerance* icon.

I also have friends whom I've built relationships with over the years who I can call and talk to about what just happened to me, or maybe we just talk about nothing in particular. If I can't reach someone to talk to, then I just talk to myself. Talking to yourself is a really good way to slow your thoughts way down, and you have to listen, because, well, it is you who is talking and you really can't go anywhere to get away from yourself. If that doesn't seem to work very well, I start writing out what just happened to me and why I am upset. That really slows your thought processes down even further, which allows you to activate your frontal lobes.

When I travel, I purposely engage with the people who look different from me while I am waiting at the airport. I might also purposely leave my house to see people who are not like me.

All of these activities will rewire my brain back to the way I want it.

If I did not understand the neurological principles I address in this book, I would not know what to do when I am treated badly by anyone who looks different from me.

That is also why every attendee who comes to my Five Skills of Tolerance training develops their own Personal Project Plan to help rewire themselves. I rarely see diversity trainers take this approach, but they should. This is a vital part of the program that is designed to ensure that the training transfers to the workplace and the individual can begin their own personal rewiring process beyond the classroom.

STEP FOUR:
Make It Part of Everyday Culture, Reward, and Enforce It

And finally, the organization's leadership must walk the walk. The worst thing that can happen is that management only pays this program lip service. The program must become a part of the organization's everyday culture. It has to be coached, modeled, and enforced.

Sad to say, most of these programs are shoved down the throats of the leadership and the employees, so no real support is ever given. In the end, the D&I program was usually done because it was the politically correct thing to do. As a result, it was never adopted as a way of daily life and so was never rewarded when it was followed. Employees were never coached when they made a mistake and no one was ever punished when these mistakes continued.

In other words, if you are going to do it ... do it right. If not, don't waste everyone's time and money. You will only do more harm than good.

6

SKILL #3: IDENTIFY & STOP BULLYING

What Is Offensive?

W e have all dealt with bullies in our lives. Whenever they are caught picking on someone, you will often hear the bully say something like, "Oh, I was just kidding," or "That's not the way I meant it," or "I don't think I was hurting them."

Unfortunately, not only do we have way too many bullies in today's world, but many of them are also just good old-fashioned hypersensitive bullies. As I have discovered first-hand, you can't say anything today without someone somewhere somehow getting offended. Then, when a hypersensitive person is offended, which happens many times a day because they are hypersensitive, that person will often attack you like a starving dog after a bone. It is an impossible situation ... and it is all bullying.

> **Yes, attacking someone over a hypersensitive issue is just another form of bullying.**

Hypersensitive bullies typically think the whole world revolves around them. They think they have the right to never be offended by anything, and they draw all kinds of attention to themselves whenever someone dares to say or do anything that offends them.

But then, how can you instantly spot a bully? How will you know when someone is really being hypersensitive? How can you tell if something is truly offensive?

Well, if you ever asked yourself these questions, you are in luck. About 30 years ago, the United States Supreme Court gave us a very real-world test that we still use to this day. Interestingly, we have all been living under this standard since 1993, even though most people don't know it. Well, it is time you did.

In *Harris v. Forklift Systems,* a female manager, Teresa Harris, was the target of many unwanted sexual comments and offensive innuendoes from Charles Hardy, the company president. (Yes, Charles Hardy was the Matt Lauer of his day.)

For instance, Hardy would suggest that he and Harris go to the Holiday Inn and negotiate her raise. He would also ask Harris and other female employees to reach deep into his front pants pocket and grab some coins for the Coke machine. He would call her a dumb-ass woman. Hardy would also throw objects on the ground in front of Harris and other female employees, order them to pick them up and then make "um, um, um!" sounds as he stared right at their backsides.

The final straw came after Harris secured a large order from a new client and she introduced the new customer to Hardy. Hardy looked at the customer, then at Harris, and asked her, "What did you do, promise the guy ... some [sex] Saturday night?"

Teresa Harris sued Forklift Systems and the case made it all the way to the United States Supreme Court.

In his defense, Charles Hardy argued that Teresa Harris was just being hypersensitive. Hardy claimed that everyone knew he was just kidding and that no one else was offended by his antics. Therefore, the question Charles Hardy posed to the Court was:

> **"Is the law going to protect hypersensitive people?"**

The U.S. Supreme Court responded by saying "no." Hypersensitive people will not be protected under the law. But then, how do you know the difference between someone who is being hypersensitive and someone who has been legitimately harassed or discriminated against? Was the harasser's conduct truly offensive or not? This is the test the Court gave us, which is still in effect today: "Would the REASONABLE PERSON in the community be offended?"

If the answer to this question is "yes," then the conduct committed by the harasser is offensive because most people in the community agree with the victim. That means you did something that most people would see as being offensive, so you need to re-examine what you are doing.

But if the answer to this question is "no," then the victim's claim has no merit. The victim is being hypersensitive because most people in the community would **not** agree that the conduct was offensive. In other words, a hypersensitive person is outside the norm of what everyone else thinks. Since most people would not be offended by what happened, the person stands apart from everyone else. By definition, they are HYPER-sensitive.

So, according to the Supreme Court, just because you're offended does not mean you're right. And yes, some people are so narcissistic that no one can ever disagree with them.

But in *Harris*, the Court ruled that the reasonable person in the community would have been very offended by Charles Hardy's conduct. So, Teresa Harris was not being hypersensitive. She had a legitimate complaint regarding Charles Hardy's behavior.

Now, it is important to note that the standard for what is offensive is very different from what constitutes an illegal hostile environment of harassment. However, that is a topic for another book. For our purposes, we will just focus on what is offensive.

At this point, we would go back to Charles Hardy and tell him that he is a pervert. Charles would probably disagree and tell us he is not a pervert because he was only kidding.

We would then correct Charles and tell him, "Oh, no. You're a pervert. We all voted."

That is how the test works. If most people in the community agree that the conduct is offensive, then it is.

Of course, some people in the community, including the bully, would agree with Charles Hardy and argue that he was only kidding. They might also argue that Teresa Harris took it all wrong or they would make up some other excuse to minimize the offensive behavior. But then, that is not the test.

The test asks, "What would *most* people in the community think?" not "What would *some* people in the community think?"

You should also notice that this test does not ask the bully's opinion or what the bully intended. Claiming that "I was only kidding" is not a relevant defense, even though I still hear that defense from every person I have ever had to coach for harassing or bullying their co-workers. All that matters is what most people think. That is all there is to it. It is very much like the court of public opinion.

However, the world has changed drastically since 1993. Back then, the local community was probably the city or state where you lived. Today, with cell phones and social media, the community has grown to encompass the country or maybe the entire world. So, in order to determine if something is truly offensive, we would ask:

> **"What would most people think**
> **if this was on the front page**
> **of *USA Today*?"**

If most people would be offended by your conduct or some comment you made, then yes, it is offensive. The problem is with you.

So, the moral of the story here is, "Don't ever do or say anything that would not look good on the front page of *USA Today*."

Of course, most people realize that maybe about 95% of everyone they meet are good, decent people. They are not bullies. Nor are they hypersensitive.

But what about the rest of the people out there, the people I call the dreaded "5 percenters"? Well, have you ever been sitting at home watching the news and at some point you just blurt out, "These people are nuts." The people you are referring to are the 5 percenters.

If the vast majority of people in the world are reasonable, then how can the bullies of the world, the 5 percenters, ruin everything for everyone else?

It is because of the real "Rules of Leadership." Now, these are not the Rules of Leadership you would learn in any college course, but these are the real rules that too many organizations follow today:

Rule #1: Never Upset Anyone.
Rule #2: Avoid All Forms Of Conflict.
Rule #3: Never Address An Issue. Ignore it. It will go away.

Unfortunately, more times than not, human resource people and management give way too much credibility to the bullies, including the hypersensitive ones, because, "Oh, no! No one should ever be offended."

This is an impossible standard and the mark of a bad leader. This is the chant of an "enabler," which is in reality the dreaded passive aggressive Retreater, the absolute worst communicator on the planet and the root cause of most of our problems. This is exactly how the bullies of the world can ruin everything for everyone.

Think about it.

I once had a client who gave everyone in the organization a $2,000.00 bonus out of the clear blue. The company had a great year, so everyone got this surprise bonus in May, just in time for summer.

Of course, most of the employees were thrilled. However, what do you think the 5 percenters thought? They were outraged. Some complained about the taxes they had to pay on the bonus. Some complained that it was not enough money. Some even complained that most of this money was going to pay their child support.

Did management make a mistake by giving the bonus? No! Of course not. But isn't that the way it goes, right? No matter what you do, some hypersensitive people will be upset. Truly bad leaders will bow down to these hypersensitive people and change what they are doing so no one will be upset.

The company's response? "If you don't like it, give it back."

The company's logic was clear: Oh, my! What would we ever do if only 95% of our employees loved what we were doing?

But then, this is what we humans do: We go right to the negative. Dr. Daniel Amen of the Amen Clinics calls these reactions ANTS, or Automatic Negative Thoughts. Of course, we humans do this because, again, in Fred Flintstone's day, it was safer for him to go to the negative. It was better to be distrusting and alive than trusting and dead. We do the same thing today, but today it is killing us.

For instance, let's say you are out on a beautiful day in a lush green meadow. In the distance, you see a real unicorn running free. You are astonished and get a picture for the *National Enquirer*. Then, winged Pegasus flies down from the sky and starts playing with the unicorn.

At that second, a hungry bear comes running out of the woods towards you. You instantly start running for the car and barely make it inside when the bear crashes into it.

Once you get home and see your family, what will you tell them all about first? Of course, it will be the bear. Even though you saw two mythical creatures, you were almost eaten by a common bear. But that is how we humans are programmed: To focus on the negative.

THAT is why so many weak leaders focus on satisfying the small minority of hypersensitive people at the expense of the 90 to 95% who are happy.

So, what do we do about this leap to the negative? We need to take that extra five seconds to stop and think. Knowing that you are a caveman or cavewoman wired to automatically react to the negative can give you that added incentive to slow down and think. REMEMBER: Unless your life really is in danger, your first reaction to a conflict is always wrong.

We will discuss the evil enablers in more detail in Chapter 8 SKILL #5: Don't Be an ENABLER!

What Is a Bully?

If I pick on you and pick on you and pick on you, that is bullying. In fact, most of us are experts in how to bully other people. Most of us earned a Ph.D. in bullying from the 12 years we spent in our public or private school systems. We bully other people in order to exalt power over someone else so we can show that we are better than that person. As a result, we move up in the social pecking order.

This is the definition of a pure bully, or what I call a **Barbarian Bully**. Klansmen, Skinheads, Neo-Nazis, and Nelson Muntz from the *Simpsons* are perfect examples of Barbarian Bullies. They love to bully other people just to boost their own self-esteem, which is usually pretty low. In other words, they think they are taller when they stand on top of more bodies.

But don't forget: Barbarian bullies are also intolerant, bigoted, emotional children.

However, the hypersensitive person who sits right next to you, that person who is offended by the slightest incident and then attacks you either to your face or behind your back over something that most people would not be upset over, can also be a Barbarian bully. They routinely think no one should ever offend them and that everyone should bow to their whim. As a result, most people have to walk around them on eggshells, afraid to make even the slightest mistake. People who respond in such a manner are, in reality, emotional children who are very intolerant of anyone else's opinion. They do not use their EPR skills and address the offense, which is the way an emotionally mature person should respond. The sad part is that we usually let them get away with it because, well, "No one should ever be offended."

Spotting any type of Barbarian bully is easy. You simply ask the question given to us by the U.S. Supreme Court: "What would most people think if this was on the front page of *USA Today*?"

There are also two other types of bullies, which are based on our fight or flight system. The first, and the most prominent one, is the passive aggressive **Angel Bully**. This is the Retreater who smiles to your face, and then stabs you in the back when you turn around. Of course, they do this to be nice. They don't want to hurt your feelings, so they simply lie to your face until you walk away. These are also the enablers of the world.

The other bully is the little attacking Devil, or the **Attacker Bully**. These are the stereotypical Simon Cowell's of the world who love to "tell it like it is" as they rip your face off. These people will also say, "Hey, I am just being honest," as they attack you to boost their own ego.

These are the three different types of bullies we all encounter, and they show everyone that it is not safe to come to work here. They destroy your trust. It is vital that you spot them and call them out when they are doing it. Of course, overcoming our natural instincts to communicate like Attackers, Retreaters or to exalt over someone like Barbarians takes a high level of emotional intelligence.

But what if I pick on you and pick on you and pick on you because of your race, religion, age, sex, sexual orientation, or gender identity? Well, that is what we call harassment because I am doing it for an illegal reason.

> **The only difference between harassment and bullying is a legal one.**

But the end result is the same: a toxic work environment and a lack of trust. No matter what you call it, it is all still just good old-fashioned bullying.

Then think about this: Who gets picked on?

People who are different from us, right? We don't pick on people who like us, and we certainly don't pick on people who are like us. We pick on people because they are different from us or because they disagree with us, which is an uncontrolled ego and emotion issue. We pick on people because of their religion, race, age, sex, height, weight or just because they are a good, old-fashioned odd duck. (What is odd? Anything different from me.)

How Widespread Is Bullying?

Again, bullying, harassment, intolerance, being an emotional child, and bigotry are all the same things. If you show me a bully, I will show you a harasser, someone who is intolerant, an emotional child, and a bigot. These are all synonyms. It really is just that simple and our society is getting worse, which then flows right into the workplace the very next day.

In fact:

- According to the *New York Daily News*, about 70% of American workers are miserable at work.[133]
- Staff Squared reports that 85% of employees hate their jobs.[134]
- Gallup Poll reported that only 30% of all American workers are engaged when they go to work every day and that the way we manage employees today is 30 years out of date.[135]
- And, under normal conditions, according to OSHA, or the U. S. Occupational Safety and Health Administration, there are over 38,000 physical assaults that occur every

week in American workplaces and we average about two homicides every workday.[136]

Of all the mammal species on the planet, humans are seven times more likely to kill one of their own. Yes, according to Dr. Douglas Fields, neuroscientist and Chief of the Nervous System Development and Plasticity Section at the National Institutes of Health, we humans are genetically predisposed to kill each other. We humans are the most homicidal mammal on earth.[137]

Of course, a great question to ask at this point is why? Why are our workplaces so caustic? Well, according to various surveys, including those conducted by CareerBuilder.com and Scott Hunter, author of *Making Work Work* (Hunter Alliance Press, 2003), the number one reason Americans hate their jobs are: Bullies.

When it is not safe to speak up in a civil manner and disagree with someone, there is no trust, and that is just another type of bullying. It all gets back to trust, and at least 70% of Americans feel they do not have that when they go into work every day.

Of course, it is not really the bullies who are the problem here. Instead, this is where the real evil of the enablers comes into play. Since "no one should ever be offended," or perhaps because the so-called leader is a passive aggressive Retreater and cannot handle conflict, the bullying and/or hypersensitive complaining is allowed to continue.

In the end, we get what we have today. Toxic workplaces where the vast majority of employees are miserable and hate going into work.

This has to stop.

Positive and Negative Intent

To many people, it seems like we are becoming a more intolerant society. Of course, people in positions of power have often been very intolerant in order to secure and maintain power. There is nothing new about that.

However, what seems to be different today are the number of common individuals who also feel this quest for control and power, which often leads to heightened levels of intolerance with disastrous results. Consider the following:

- Statista reported that school shootings have increased from 20 per year in 1970 to 112 in 2020, which equates to over three shootings a week during a normal school year.
- The FBI reported that hate crimes in America in 2020 were the highest they had been in over a decade.
- The Southern Poverty Law Center reports that the number of hate groups in America has doubled in the last 20 years.

Part of this intolerant culture is the *Hang 'Em High* mentality we seem to be fostering whenever someone disagrees with us. It ranges from attacking someone when they simply disagree with us, to joining hate groups when someone is different from us, to actually killing people who have offended us in some way.

We do not use our EPR skills to discuss those issues that bother us. We don't engage in a dialogue with the other person to find out what they meant by what they did or said. Even if the person sees they made a mistake and apologizes, we still tend to go right to the Clint Eastwood *Hang 'Em High* type of mentality rather than trying to reform the person. (I always wondered about that expression. If you hang someone one inch, they are just as dead as if you hang someone 10 feet. I think the extra 9 feet 11 inches is just for fun ... or for show. In the end, it is meant to send a message of fear.)

As a result, too many of us instantly think that the person who simply disagreed with us did so with a negative intent, which is not necessarily the case. We think they are trying to get us. We rarely stop and think that this person simply has an opinion that differs from ours, and that is OK.

More disturbing is the fact that we instantly dehumanize the person who just dared to disagree with us or offend us, so we completely ignore the fact that this is another human being, someone with feelings and emotions, just like you and me. We forget we might need to forgive this person, or maybe, just maybe, we are wrong because we did not take the time to use our EPR skills to understand what this person was saying or where this person was coming from. Every major religion on the planet requires us to exercise our humanity, but millions of seemingly religious people have taken out their imaginary X-ACTO knives and excised those passages from their religious texts. That is one reason why we have so many people who violate their religions and commit great crimes against their fellow human beings.

Unfortunately, many of the people who pray the loudest do not want to worship God, they want to become God. They want the power to smite anyone who disagrees with them. I will often have such people tell me how religious they are, even though they break the basic requirements of their faith every day. To that, I always reply, "Well, I sure am glad you told me how devout you are because I would have never guessed it by the way you act."

Of course, that also explains why God also made Hell.

What Is Cancel Culture?

I recently had a client who suspended a manager for mistakenly referring to a transgender employee by the wrong pronoun. Since this person was transgender, he identified as a male, even though he was biologically born a female. He was not undergoing any type of gender reassignment, which would have made him transexual. Instead, he simply stopped wearing makeup, cut his hair short and he wore golf shirts and jeans. When the manager forgot and referred to this employee as a "she" and not a "he," the employee filed a written complaint with the company. The manager admitted to referring to the employee by the wrong pronoun. The manager said he forgot and quickly apologized. Still, the company suspended the manager because the transgender employee was upset. The company claimed it was enforcing its zero tolerance policy, even though the EEOC found in 2016 that such policies do more harm than good since too many companies fail to look at the facts of each individual case. This is the *Hang 'Em High* mentality we are fostering whenever someone makes even the simplest of mistakes, even when the person shows true repentance. This is what some refer to as the "cancel culture."

On February 4, 2021, CBS This Morning reported that Morgan Wallen, a 27-year-old rising country music superstar, was caught on video using the n-word after a night of partying. The backlash was swift and severe. Many country fans and media critics expressed disappointment with his actions and welcomed the consequences. The Country Music Association removed all of his content from their platforms, the Academy of Country Music said Wallen was no longer eligible for its upcoming awards ceremony and his contract was suspended by his record label, although what that meant exactly was not clear.

Wallen has since released a series of apologies, including a five-minute Instagram video where he admits what he did, how wrong it was and how he pledged to "be better." He also asked that he be allowed to "take ownership for this" and "accept any penalties" that are coming his way.

Was Wallen sincere in his apologies? Who knows? Should Wallen suffer consequences for what he did? Absolutely. Should we "Hang Him High" and cancel his life?

Mickey Guyton, a Black female country western star, perhaps put it best. Guyton, who was very critical of Wallen and the culture of the country music industry itself, posted on her Twitter account, "And lastly, I do not believe in cancel culture. Watching anyone fall from grace is a terrible thing to see. People must all be given a chance to change. Morgan must feel the weight of his words but completely throwing someone away is detrimental to anyone's mental health."

People are not disposable. They can reform. Everyone makes mistakes. Hanging Morgan Wallace high will only result in more boomerang bigotry. Remember: We all need to rewire ourselves and change. Perhaps, just perhaps, this experience will make Wallace one of the best spokespeople for racial change, much like Frank Meekins' experiences reformed him from a violent Skinhead into one of the best advocates for tolerance in this country, as you will see later in this book.

Again, we all make mistakes, as you see in the news every day. Let's keep our humanity for the sake of ourselves and others.

Sadly, this is not typically what we do today. Instead, if someone disagrees with us, or if someone maybe offends us in some way, most people do not address the situation with the person, use their EPR skills, and try to resolve the issue. Too many of us go right into caveman or cavewoman mode and either openly attack the person, or more than likely, take the "nice" passive aggressive approach and stab them in the back ... never giving the other person any chance to explain their side. Yes, our base instincts buy right into the cancel culture or the *Hang 'Em High* mentality.

Again, when someone strikes you down, do you really care if the blow came from the left or the right?

This is what I saw with the accounting firm and its CPAs, but it also happens with far too many human resource associations. It never ceases to amaze me how often I have voiced an opinion to some HR association, have them disagree with me, but never tell me about it. Instead, they scurry behind my back and never talk to me again. This is particularly disturbing because HR professionals are supposed to be the experts at coaching employees and resolving conflicts, but this is the example many of the people leading these associations set for their members. It perpetuates the worst stereotypes about human resources.

Of course, this passive aggressive approach does nothing but enable the bullies of the world, which will destroy any D&I program they ever try to implement.

> **This is why you cannot be in a leadership, HR, or any D&I position if you are passive aggressive. It is the definition of enabling evil.**

Why is being a passive aggressive evil? Because bullies, hypersensitive people, and bigots always complain when they are confronted with their behavior. Passive aggressive Retreaters do nothing but enable the bigots to continue ruling over their "Kingdoms of Nod," which are the lands they reign over through terror. Believe me, when up to 85% of all employees say they are miserable at work, we have some people who need upsetting.

Consider the instance of Melissa Click, Assistant Professor of Communication at the University of Missouri. On November 10, 2015, Click was protesting a series of racist incidents that occurred on the University of Missouri campus when a photojournalist student, Tim Tai, was photographing the event. Click's immediate response, which was caught on video, was to verbally attack Tai, even calling for "some muscle" to come over and physically remove him from the area.[138]

This video has gone viral, in case you would like to Google it, and see a real-life college professor acting like a three-year-old child.

What I wonder most about this situation is why did Click go right to the negative and attack Tim Tai? I would think if you were going to stage a protest, you would want some photojournalists and press to show up and cover the event. I mean, if no one really knows you are there and why you are conducting this rally, why bother?

However, Click's reaction stunned the world. Why didn't she think, "Oh, good! Here is a photojournalist. I'll bet he can help get us the coverage we want." Or if she was unsure of his intent, why didn't she just use her EPR skills and ask him what he was doing? Of course, she was not able to use her EPR skills to resolve the conflict because she was too busy melting down. This emotional temper tantrum cost Click her job and severely damaged her reputation forever.

Of all the options available to her, she chose the worst. And yes, please do not miss the irony here. She is a communication professor. (My undergraduate degree is actually in Organizational Communication and this is not what they taught me at Ohio State.)

Again, whenever I see sad situations like this, I can't help but wonder: If Dr. Click had known about the Five Skills of Tolerance, would this not have happened to her? She would have known what was in her subconscious and she would have been able to rewire it long before this incident occurred. She would have also understood more about her fight or flight response and that she was about to fly into a rage, which would be bad for her. She could have taken that critical five extra seconds to slow down and let her frontal lobes catch up, or she could have just walked away for a bit. I don't think it ever dawned on her that she was a bullying, intolerant, bigoted, emotional child, just like the rest of us. Maybe, just maybe, she wouldn't have destroyed her reputation if she had this skill set.

Was her cause just? Yes, of course. She was protesting the racist incidents that occurred in her own backyard. Did she have a right to protest? Absolutely. Did she have the right to attack Tim Tai because she felt her cause was justified? Not at all. But this happens to many of us, conservatives and liberals alike. If I feel I am right in what I am doing, if I am on a Blues Brothers' Mission from God, I now have the moral right to rip you to pieces. Right? (Insert evil smile here.)

Did she make a mistake? Yes, a huge mistake. But then, isn't she human? Have you ever done something stupid and just "lost it"? Were you lucky enough to *not* be recorded doing it? Did Dr. Click deserve to be cancelled or to be "Hung High"? Did she understand the mistake that she made and was she willing to apologize and reform? Yes, and she did that, both to Tim Tai privately and in public, but it didn't seem to make any difference. The decision was made to cancel her, as she soon lost her job at the university.

Of course, some things that people do are beyond redemption, but those situations tend to be at the extreme. Most of what we cancel people for these days are for offenses we all commit at one time or another. That is when we all need to be more tolerant and take a look at helping the person redeem themselves.

Of course, I doubt this was the first time Dr. Click ever had such an emotional meltdown. I always think about the passive aggressive people in her life, particularly her friends and her superiors. Did anyone do her any favors by not using their EPR skills and addressing this type of behavior with her? Were they doing their jobs? Were they being nice? If someone really was her friend, addressing this overzealous behavior with Dr. Click would have been the nice thing to do ... and it might have saved her career.

Again, that is exactly what we humans do: We go right to the negative. Taking those extra five seconds to stop and think can really save your life.

Being a presenter, I will conduct seminars on very sensitive topics, like bullying, tolerance, and so on. It is becoming more and more common that I get someone in the audience, maybe a few people, ready to attack me. They can't wait to show everyone that they are the sentinel of decency by attacking a White bigot, or so they think.

In one instance, I was conducting a seminar on tolerance and the subject of segregation came up. One of the attendees said that America's history with Black segregation was the worst the world has ever seen, especially under the guise of separate but equal laws, or Jim Crow.

I told him I understood where he was coming from, and that part of American history is something we should never forget, lest we ever repeat those mistakes. However, world history is full of these types of segregation laws, such as in South Africa with apartheid and in Nazi Germany with the Warsaw Ghetto.

As soon as the word "ghetto" came out of my mouth, three or four young Black attendees launched their attack. They instantly lashed out at me for using a racist term like "ghetto." Of course, since I am a White guy, I must also be a racist, right?

Now, I have been attacked over many things in my career, but this one really caught me off guard. I asked them what was racist about the Warsaw Ghetto?

They told me the word "ghetto" was a racist term used against Blacks. It was an offensive term and I shouldn't use it. While this is true to a certain extent, we were obviously not using the term in the same context.

Before I could even think, I replied, "Have any of you *ever* studied the Holocaust?"

They just sort of looked at each other. Apparently, they had not, but they did know that the word ghetto refers to all things bad and Black, or so they thought.

I asked them to Google the term, Warsaw Ghetto.

Actually, that is the really cool thing about leading seminars these days. The world really is at your fingertips.

Right away, they all got busy punching in their searches. You could almost hear a collective "Oh" rise from the crowd. I then asked them what they found. A few hands went up, so I called on a young woman to read what she had found.

She then read from her phone, "The Warsaw Ghetto was the largest of all the Jewish ghettos in German-occupied Europe during World War II."

"Does it say anything about black people?" I asked her.

"No, it doesn't," she replied.

"Are there any pictures of any black people in the ghetto?" I asked.

"No, all I see are a bunch of old White guys with beards," she replied.

"Yeah, we call them Jews," I told her. (Insert a little more sarcasm here.)

But isn't that the way it goes today? The world is only as big as what I know, and if I misinterpret something you said, I have every right to attack you. We go right to the negative, thanks to our fight or flight response. We *Hang 'Em High*.

Not one person in the room asked me what I meant by referring to the Warsaw Ghetto. No one asked me if I was referring to Blacks. No one asked for any type of clarification. Instead, they just extended their retractable claws and attacked.

Sadly, it really never occurred to most of them that I was not trying to offend anyone. Even if I had said something inappropriate, they were not going to educate me. I had offended them, and it was time for blood.

It also never occurred to these young 20-somethings that maybe, just maybe, I knew something they did not. Apparently, anything that happened before they were born was not important. Well, I have news for everyone: There are a few things that happened in the world before you and I were born. Just a few.

I have a solid rule that I follow: I try not to look stupid.

If someone offends me, or if they say something that strikes me as odd, I will ask them what they meant by that and try to not let my emotions take over. I use my EPR skills. Maybe, just maybe, another person knows something I don't and I might learn something new.

I could actually fill a whole book with these types of examples where someone has made a seemingly innocent comment without having any negative intent, but they are attacked for making it just the same. It is a truly sad situation for us all.

The real issue here is not whether someone inadvertently said something offensive. We will all do that at one point or another. It will happen to you. Whatever rules we currently have in place regarding what is acceptable to say and not will change with the next strong wind. One day, we will all get caught off guard by something that was acceptable to say yesterday, but it somehow became unacceptable to say today. It will one day happen to us all.

However, the real issue lies with the person who got terribly offended by the comment. Do we assume the person who offended us had a positive intent with what they said ... or do we go right for the throat and instantly assume that the comment was made with negative intent, so it is OK to start crucifying the person right away?

REMEMBER: Unless your life is truly in danger, your first reaction to a conflict is always wrong. It is wrong because our first reaction always reverts to fight or flight, and in the 21st century, that could be really bad for you.

We need to stop allowing our caveman and cavewoman impulses to control us, which takes us right to our negative intent. Whenever we do that, we tend to cancel the other person because they might have made a mistake.

We all have to stop doing that. Instead, we need to take a breath, slow down, take that critical five seconds for our frontal lobes to gain control over our emotional response, and use our EPR skills to address the problem. If you cannot gain control of yourself at that moment, then walk away. Otherwise, you might be the next person who gets cancelled or "Hung High" by social media, as we have seen happen so many times already.

No, we have not evolved at all. We are still cavemen and cavewomen in pants, but we need to start doing better.

Bullying Is About Power ... and Fear

Far too many of us really love our bigotry and our bullying behavior. We love it! We wrap ourselves in it like Linus' blanket.

Actually, if a bully would tell you the truth, they would say something like:

> "I don't want to get rid of my bigotry. Why would I ever want to do that? In order to feel better about myself, I have to believe that you are *not* my equal. I have to believe that I am better than you! Therefore, I use my bigotry to feed my diminished ego, which is an emotional intelligence issue. As a result of this artificial sense of superiority ... I grant myself the right to be intolerant of you and your differences. But then, I am still a good person and I know I am better than you because ... well... I AM BETTER THAN YOU!"

(Wonderful circular reasoning, don't you think?)
This process can all be diagrammed as follows:

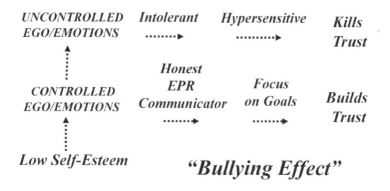

As you can see in this diagram, someone with low self-esteem starts at the bottom. They do not feel good about themselves, so they want to raise their own feelings of self-worth. But rather than raising their self-esteem through their own accomplishments and controlling their ego and emotions, they put the pedal to the metal and shoot to the top of the model. They overcompensate.

As a result, they now have uncontrolled emotions and ego because they are constantly trying to hide from everyone that they really feel inadequate. Their fragile ego cannot take anyone disagreeing with them, so their emotions take over and they become very intolerant of anyone who disagrees with them, which makes them hypersensitive to even the smallest slights.

Of course, there are some people who start at the top of the model. They are narcissists and think they are better than everyone else, so the normal rules of common decency do not apply to them. In other words, they just get too big for their britches. They are emotional children, which means they never even got to first base.

In the end, no one is safe from such vicious attacks, so the trust and the free flow of information in the organization is destroyed. This is how we end up engaging in the absolute worst kind of behavior and make the worst decisions that can result in blowing space shuttles out of the air.

This is important to remember because racism is not about race, sexism is not about sex, ageism is not about age, and so on. Instead, bigotry and egocentrism are all about one thing:

> **POWER ... Nothing more ...
> Nothing less.**

This power and a desire to feel superior over others grants us the moral permission to bully another person because "You just can't trust those people," or "He is an idiot anyway," or "They are just animals." This is the act of dehumanizing others.

Dehumanization

For a sane human being to severely bully another person, we must first dehumanize that person. Once we dehumanize this person, we can do anything we want to them because they are no longer a human being like you, me, and anyone else we let into our in-group.

We dehumanize groups of people because we want to exalt power over them, which is also done to boost our own low self-esteem. Oftentimes, however, there is something else at work here:

> **We are afraid of
> "those other people."**

That creates a lethal situation, and it is all downhill after that.

Whenever we see "all those people" as being dangerous to us, we need to get them before they get us. We are protecting our way of life, our families, and ourselves. This pattern has repeated itself throughout all human history. Again, this is your typical boomerang bigotry, or competitive victimization.

When we dehumanize others, we are denying that "those people" are fully human. It is not something that happens instantaneously, like flipping a switch. Instead, it is a slow and gradual process that actually changes the way our brain fires in relation to these other people. As we previously discussed in the *SKILL #2: Overcome Your Subconscious Brain & Resolve Conflict (EPR)* chapter, we can actually change how our brain operates and how it is wired to conform to the belief system we are adopting. Yes, our brain will physically change the way it is wired to adapt to the environment we subject it to every

171

day. Also, today's research shows that over time, this desensitization towards others will actually turn off parts of our brain that allow us to empathize with "those people."[139]

> **In other words, whatever you think ... you will become.**

Normally, whenever we empathize with others, one part of our brain that is activated is a section in our frontal lobes, or more precisely, in our medial prefrontal cortex. That part of the brain is largely responsible for our social cognition and it is visible to researchers. Researchers have shown that we humans will actually demonstrate less activity in this area of the brain when we dehumanize others over time. Eventually, we do not think about these other people as being human at all. We see these other people as lacking the basic characteristics commonly attributed to human beings, such as having certain mental capacities.[140] They are part of the out-group, and, of course, we are part of the in-group. So, in order to protect our in-group, we feel perfectly justified in doing whatever we want to do to "those people."[141]

Yes, today, we can actually see bigotry function in someone's brain.

Dehumanization is a common technique used to incite not just bullying, or even harassment, but it is part of the playbook for every act of genocide the world has ever known.[142]

You can always spot the dehumanization of others by the rhetoric we use. We refer to those people as animals, vermin, rats, rapists, killers, murders, drug users, and so on. You will also see it in the symbols we use, such as those used by the various hate groups. Yes, this rhetoric and these symbols are powerful ... and they can be very dangerous.[143]

This dehumanization process was used to perpetuate the Rwandan genocide in 1994. Back when Rwanda was a colony under Belgium in the 1900s, the people of Rwanda were very united. To better control the people, Belgium needed a way to separate and divide them. As a result, if you owned more than ten cows, you were classified as a Tutsi. If you had fewer than ten cows, then you were classified as a Hutu. In 1935, the government issued cards that actually identified everyone according to these arbitrary classifications: Hutu or Tutsi.[144]

In 1994, the Hutu government launched a media attack against the outcast and minority Tutsis. Popular slogans used by the Hutu media were "No cockroach ever gave birth to a butterfly" and "What weapons shall we use to conquer the cockroaches once and for all?" Everyone was encouraged to use weapons in their attacks against the Tutsis.[145]

The radio would blast out constant messages like, "Notice to all cockroaches" and they would refer to the Tutsi people as "snakes." This was all motivated by a Hutu agenda to gain political power. In the end, over 1,000,000 people were murdered.[146]

Martin Buber perhaps summarized the entire issue of dehumanization best. In Buber's "philosophy of dialogue," he focused on the distinction between the relationship of the "I and It." In short, Buber concluded:[147]

> **"Objectification" occurs whenever**
> **I change someone from a**
> **"*YOU*" to an "*IT*."**

It is so simple it is brilliant. As soon as I turn you into an object, as soon as I dehumanize you, I can bully you, I can harass you, I can discriminate against you and I can even kill you because you are no longer a human being. I can then feel pretty good about what I have done because a big part of the dehumanization process is that this out-group poses a threat to me and my family. There is no trust because it is not safe to have this out-group around. The mere fact that I might have to kill a few of those people, or even millions of "those Jews," is a good thing. My actions are justified because my family is safer now.

Have you ever wondered why so many people would go to see someone being lynched, whether it be a Black man, a Jew, a Native American, or a White man, and they would actually pose in front of the dead body to have their picture taken? Dehumanization and objectification play a significant part in that. They have killed "that animal" before they or their family became victims. They think they actually just did a good thing for their community. Simple.

Dehumanization gives us all the permission we need to openly be bullying, intolerant, bigoted, emotional children ... and still feel pretty good about ourselves.

Time and neuroscience have done nothing but prove the words of Elie Wiesel, Nobel Peace Prize winner and Holocaust survivor, to be prophetic:

"Hatred is a cancer that is passed from one person to another, one people to another."[148]

Recently, researchers have been studying a form of this dehumanization called "blatant dehumanization." In researching how far our dehumanization of others goes, participants were asked to rate the degree of humanization they assign to different groups of people according to the following dehumanization scale.[149]

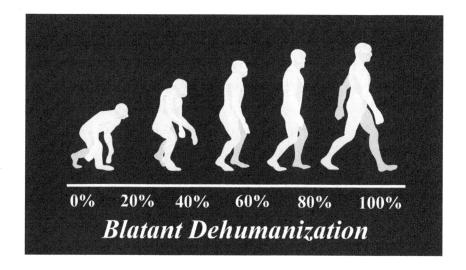

These studies have been startling. For instance, we Americans typically see ourselves as being pretty close to 100% human. However, many of us see Mexican immigrants as only being about 75% human. The British, Danish, Greek and Spanish participants saw Muslims as being only about 60% human.[150]

Whenever we see a group of people as lacking certain qualities that we feel are essential to being fully human, we rank them lower on the humanization scale. We therefore see these people as not being like us, but instead we describe them as being barbaric, savages, lacking in morals, aggressive, primitive, irresponsible, cold-hearted, and backward, to mention a few.[151]

This dehumanization of others has increased in recent years thanks to the internet. Facebook and search engines like Google use algorithms to track where you go on the internet so they can then forward ads and other websites to you that match your interests. On the surface, this might sound fine. Actually, I kind of like it whenever I Google something like "Fun things to do this summer." I will get many sites sent to me that help me with my search. Whenever I am looking for something to buy, like waterproof tarps for my backyard, I will get many ads popping up in my margins showing me good tarps for sale at good prices. I mean, this is like having my own personal shopper. What could be wrong with that?[152]

Well, if you want to see the problem, try Googling something like, "Good things Hitler did," or "Why Stalin was a good guy," and so on. Pretty soon, those algorithms will start steering many of these hate group websites and ads to you. It will feed your bigotry and your biases with each additional search. Pretty soon, you will be inundated by these types of sites, many of which disguise their bigotry in very clever ways. Actually, after doing this for a while, you will not even have to search for these hate sites. They will just come to you with most any search you do. In the end, you will begin to think that this type of hateful propaganda is normal. In reality, you are starting to rewire your brain in a very dangerous way.[153]

Does this mean search engines like Google are evil? Of course not. Search engines are like anything else in this world. They can be good and they can be bad depending on what you do with them. We humans have to be aware of their positive and negative uses so we can control how we use them. It is like owning a car. Are cars evil because they kill so many people every year? Not at all. A car can be a very good thing if you can control it. It will destroy you if you cannot.

Before the internet, it was much more difficult to find someone to reinforce your radical or even violent beliefs. People who shared these ideas were often miles or maybe even continents away from each other. Today, it is easy to find many people who share your views on anything. These internet tools are actually designed to do just that: Reinforce your beliefs. Remember confirmation bias?

The internet is a very effective tool in priming the beliefs you already hold and want to reinforce, which can greatly amplify someone's misinformed projection of the world. It is classic confirmation bias gone digital.[154]

This modern-day phenomenon was a critical factor in forming Dylann Roof's view of the world. If you recall, on June 17, 2015, Roof, a White supremacist, went into a Bible study group at the Emanuel African Methodist Church and opened fire, killing nine African Americans and wounding another.[155]

When he was later interrogated by police, Roof said that he had just killed a few people. He then told police:[156]

- "Blacks are killing White people in the streets every day."
- "Somebody had to do something."
- "They rape 100 White women a day."
- "What I did was miniscule to what they are doing to White people every day."

Roof admitted that his true motive was to agitate race relations and bring about a civil race war.

But where did he get all of this misinformation? Actually, Roof's internet trails were telling. After the Trayvon Martin and George Zimmerman story broke, Roof became interested in learning more about the crimes committed by Blacks against Whites. Thinking he was doing his homework on the topic, he searched "Black on White crime" on Google. From this search, Roof found many websites that gave him exactly what he wanted to see: Websites professing that Black on White crime was out of control in this country.[157]

Roof's search gave him several cloaked websites, all of which looked very respectable and credible on the surface, but when you looked further, they were run by White supremacists. These cloaked websites use fear to motivate anyone who reads their materials. They focus their message on the oppression and physical peril of White people. They prime the fight or flight response of White people by making them afraid of Black people, or maybe Mexican immigrants, or gays or just about anyone else they don't like that week.

These websites can do a couple of things to us. First, when we see upsetting news, we typically do not slow down and think about what we are reading. The headlines are designed to get us to react emotionally to what we see, especially when the emotion is related to fear, and that is usually a bad way to form an opinion or make decisions. Whenever emotions are involved, we tend to react first ... and think later. Again, using that critical five seconds to stop and think can save us from ourselves.

Next, over time, these websites can literally rewire our brains in a very dangerous way. These websites can reinforce the worst of what we already think or they can also change the way we view the world, especially when an element of fear is involved. Remember, studies have shown that we humans can begin to rewire our brains in as little as 15 minutes.

This is what happened to Dylann Roof, or rather this is how Dylann Roof allowed the Internet to shape his world view.[158]

According to federal prosecutors, Roof was entirely self-radicalized online. Roof did not have any "personal associations or experiences with White supremacist groups or individuals or others" to influence his radical beliefs. He did not need them. He had the internet search engines.[159]

Of course, this is no excuse for what Roof did. He chose to visit those websites, which caused him to react emotionally and also rewired his brain, to one degree or another. He did it to himself. The real issue here is that Roof's self-radicalization did not require any human interaction from anyone, which happens to millions of people every day.

Of course, none of what Roof believed was supported by any official source, such as by the FBI's crime statistics. According to the FBI, most acts of violence committed by African Americans are directed against other Blacks. Violent Black on Black crime is actually much more prevalent than Black on White.[160]

However, just as important as these algorithms is the fact that search engines like Google are also advertising websites. Websites can pay these search engines to get a better ranking on your searches. Whenever we conduct a search, it looks like we are going to the library and picking out what we want to see, so it has our trust. But that is not always true. Instead, we often see many of the websites sponsors have paid for us to see, in addition to what the algorithms produce for us.[161]

Yes, the internet is a double-edged sword. It has never been easier to keep yourself informed and research the issues of the day. However, it has also never been easier to misinform everyone as well.[162]

So, what do we do about this? First and foremost: SLOW DOWN AND THINK!

Again, our emotions will commandeer our brains in 17,000ths of a second. If you do not slow down, control your emotional brain and use your frontal lobes, you might start to believe this hateful and dehumanizing rhetoric.

It is the same thing as thinking that cows drink milk.

Then, rewire, rewire, rewire! We all need to be very cognizant of what information we are sending to our brains. Just as you would not want to sit in a room and breathe in toxic fumes, you do not ever want to expose your brain to a toxic environment. You need to protect your brain just as you would any other part of your body.

Dealing with Bullies

Today, our fight or flight response is reinforced and stimulated more than ever before in history. Additionally, our society reinforces the desire to attack anyone who opposes us with our *Hang 'Em High* mentality. The more right we feel we are, or the more danger we sense from "all those people," the louder we tend to yell at them. Yes, this is human nature, but today it is being catapulted forward at a lethal pace.

How quickly we have forgotten the message of David Henry Thoreau, the father of civil disobedience. Strong but peaceful protests were the key to civil disobedience that changed the hearts of men and women everywhere, and then changed the world. In fact, Thoreau's writings did change the world because they first individually influenced the thoughts and beliefs of such people as Leo Tolstoy, Mahatma Gandhi, and Martin Luther King, Jr.

That is how lasting change has always worked. You start with motivating individual people to want to change, and the world's institutions will soon follow.

John Lewis' message of "good trouble" was the perfect response to such injustices as Rodney King and George Floyd. Lewis' message of encouraging everyone to engage in civil disobedience in a strong, brave, and peaceful manner was a great one, but human instinct gets the better of us too many times. Protesting in such a peaceful but strong manner is simply too hard for many of us human beings.

Thoreau understood human nature. He understood that attacking another human gets you nothing but the old blow-up punching bag phenomenon. The harder you hit it, the harder it hits you back.

Actually, when considering human behavior, Jesus' teaching of "turn the other cheek" makes perfect sense. It is not just philosophical; it is practical and highly effective when dealing with human beings.

You actually see this type of punching bag effect on the news almost every day. For example, the next time you go to your local Neo-Nazi rally, you will see the White supremacists show up with their hate messages and often yelling all kinds of obscene things into the crowd. On the other side, you will see the anti-protestors screaming and yelling right back at the White supremacists. In the end, you have both sides yelling and screaming at each other with the police caught in the middle, often trying to keep everyone from killing each other.

Again, this is boomerang bigotry coming back to get you.

It's all too sad to watch. It would make Thoreau cry.

All this attacking does is strengthen the other side's resolve. It proves to each side that those opposing them are nothing but animals.

Of course, with competitive victimization, we excuse our own vile behavior because, well, "They started it."

With tensions heightened to that level, all it takes is a micro-nudge for the entire situation to erupt into a riot. And then everyone loses.

Again, since we only have one emotional system, our brain does not recognize the difference between someone punching us in the face and someone yelling at us. All our emotional system and amygdala know is that we are in danger, so our fight or flight response becomes engaged at 17,000ths of a second. This phenomenon is called "endangerment."[163]

Consequently, every time you yell at someone, demean them, or insult them, it is the same as punching them in the gut as far as their fight or flight system is concerned.

Now you know why these situations so often turn violent.

My favorite example of how to properly deal with a bully is from Frank Meeink. His book, *Autobiography of a Recovering Skinhead*, was actually the premise of the movie, *American History X*. Yes, Frank's story is all true.

Frank Meeink was born in South Philadelphia. From his earliest days, he had no relationship with his biological father. His relationship with his mother, who abused drugs and alcohol, was not much better.[164]

As a teenager, Meeink was bullied at school because he was White. His Black schoolmates would taunt him hoping he would react so they could beat him up and claim that he started it. To Frank, it seemed that the entire Black community was doing this to him.[165]

When he was thirteen, Frank's cousin took him to Lancaster, Pennsylvania where he met his first group of Neo-Nazis. They accepted him. This was his safe place and they actually talked to Frank about what it was like to be him. That had never happened to him before in his life. They became his family, the only real family he really ever had. That was when he joined the Neo-Nazi movement.[166]

Soon after that, Frank was traveling the country working as a Skinhead leader and a Neo-Nazi recruiter. He would go out with gangs of Neo-Nazis and beat up people at random. In Illinois, he even had his own cable-access TV show called *The Reich*.[167]

However, Frank heard that one of his rivals was trying to steal some of his recruits, and he "just couldn't have that." Frank called him up and told him they were having a neutral Christmas party and invited his rival to come on over. Of course, there wasn't any party. Frank was waiting with some of his friends to beat up the rival and teach him a lesson. Frank never thought this rival would go to the police, but he did.[168]

At 17, Frank was arrested for aggravated kidnapping. He accepted a plea bargain that gave him a mandatory sentence of three years.[169]

When Frank got out of prison three years later, no one would hire him. He had a felony conviction for aggravated kidnapping on his record with a swastika on his neck. He was an employment leper.[170]

The "good" people of the world shunned him entirely, which only reinforced Frank's bigoted beliefs. Isolated, all this mistreatment did was to force Frank into thinking about returning to his previous life.

But one of his friends found him a job. The job was working on antique furniture for an antique store. However, his friend told him there was one catch: The owner was a Jew.[171]

Frank said he didn't care as long as he didn't have to talk to him. If he could just do his job, everything would be fine.[172]

His buddy told him that the owner, Tony, knew all about Frank's past and he didn't care. Tony had only one rule: Don't break his furniture.[173]

Frank went to work for Tony, the Jew. At the end of his first week, Frank was convinced that Tony would not pay him the money he was owed. He thought for sure that Tony fit every stereotype he had ever heard about Jews, so he just knew Tony was going to "Jew" him. Frank was getting himself ready for a battle with Tony.[174]

When Tony came up to Frank at the end of the week, he asked him, "I owe you some money, don't I?"[175]

Frank immediately responded saying, "Yes, you do. You owe me some money. Yes, you do."[176]

Tony asked him, "How much do I owe you?"[177]

Frank fired right back, still convinced Tony was going to cheat him out of his money, "Three hundred dollars. It is a hundred bucks a day."[178]

"Oh, yeah. That's right. That's right," Tony replied.[179]

Tony then pulled out a huge wad of cash and counted off three one-hundred-dollar bills, "Here's one, two, and here's three ... and hold on, here's an extra hundred bucks. You're a really good worker."[180]

Frank was stunned. Not only did Tony give him a job when no one else in the world would, but Tony paid Frank an extra one hundred dollars that was not even owed to him. Tony had not "Jewed" Frank. He bonused him.

Tony then drove Frank home and asked him what he did for a living. Frank told him he didn't do anything for a living. He had a swastika on his neck.[181]

Tony then asked Frank, "Then why don't you come to work for me?"[182]

On top of everything else, Tony gave Frank a full-time job when most other people in the world were ostracizing him and ridiculing him. To most of the good people of the world, he was a low life Neo-Nazi. He was not human and worthy of their concern.[183]

Frank started working for Tony fulltime, but Frank also kept wearing his Nazi boots. He was still a Neo-Nazi.[184]

However, one day, Frank accidently broke a piece of furniture. The one rule that Tony had was to never break any of his furniture, and Frank just broke one. Frank was sure he would not only get fired, but he was convinced Tony would take the cost of the broken furniture out of his pay. Frank apologized to Tony and told him that it was a stupid mistake.[185]

Instead, Tony took Frank's pay out of his pocket and handed the whole amount over to him. Tony did not count it or take anything out for the cost of the broken furniture. He handed it all over to Frank and said, "Here you go. I'll see you Monday, right?"[186]

Frank was stunned. He said later that he felt like crying, and he still chokes up when he tells this story today. Instead, he just looked at Tony and said, "Yeah, I'll see you Monday."[187]

As soon as he got home, Frank ripped off his Nazi boots and threw them down into his mom's basement. He never wore them again.[188]

When the whole world, a world filled with good decent people, were all treating Frank like the best thing he could do with his life was to end it, it was Tony, a Jew, who befriended him. Tony changed the world a little bit by changing the life of a single person, Frank.

In Greek theater, a hero is someone who is flawed at the beginning of the play, sees his mistakes, searches his soul, and changes. That is what a hero was to the Greeks. This is one of the most beautiful stories of a hero I have ever heard in my life. That is Frank Meeink.

Frank has always been a human being. He was a human being when he was born, he was a human being when he was abused by his stepfather, he was a human being when he was bullied by the Black classmates at his school, he was a human being when he was a Neo-Nazi, and he is still a human being to this day.

Frank said when he was marching for the Neo-Nazis, people would yell and scream at them all the time. They would even throw snowballs, bottles, and bricks at them.[189]

Never once did it ever make Frank or any of his friends think, "Boy, I really need to rethink my beliefs here." Instead, the hate that was thrown at them only strengthened their bonds with each other. Someone was attacking their family and that would only bring them closer together.[190]

It was all boomerang bigotry.

However, Frank said he did not know how to defend himself against someone who was just talking to him, like Tony did. If someone yelled at him or threw a bottle at him, he knew how to respond to that. He knew how to physically fight an enemy. That was easy.

Again, whenever you ostracize or yell at a bully, as happened to Frank many times in his life, the brain registers that emotional attack the same as if it was a physical one. Again, that is endangerment. It is all the same to the human brain, and it provokes a boomerang response.[191]

But when Frank ran into the kindness of one Jew, his sworn enemy, he was left speechless.

Frank's story is the perfect example of why requiring someone to be accepting of others will not work. Such tactics would have only alienated Frank even more. Instead, when Frank met someone he was programmed to hate, a Jew, and that person treated him like a real human being, Frank's subconscious began to rewire itself. In the end, Frank became the more accepting person every diversity expert in this country wanted him to become.

Rewiring Frank's subconscious and core belief system drastically changed how he viewed the world and the people around him. Since his subconscious brain had been rewired, his implicit biases stopped, which in turn reduced his explicit biases.[192]

Frank later said on a CNN News Day interview with Christy Paul that this country desperately needs a hate intervention. He said you cannot attack someone who hates you with more hate. Frank is right, as was Thoreau.

Bullies typically feel like they have never been respected and they are under attack, which is usually why they are bullies in the first place. Attacking them all over again only repeats the same cycle. It is a self-fulfilling prophecy.

John Lewis' good trouble is the way to go.

7

SKILL #4: UNDERSTAND REAL DIFFERENCES VERSUS STEREOTYPES & MYTHS

Are there real differences between us? And if there are real differences between us, where do the real differences end and the stereotypes and myths begin? Understanding such distinctions is critical to not only eliminating these stereotypes and myths from our minds, which we also call "labeling," but it is also critical to understanding when someone is making a comment that is based on a real difference between us and when they are indeed labeling or stereotyping someone.

To illustrate this point in my seminars, I will often ask the audience some basic questions and let them decide if I am talking about a real difference between us or if I am talking about a stereotype or myth. For instance, I will ask, "Are there any REAL DIFFERENCES between men and women?"

To that, I will get a laugh from the audience and hear a resounding, "Yes."

It is obvious there are indeed real differences between men and women ... and anyone who has ever been married or divorced has witnessed these differences first-hand.

I will then ask the audience: "OK, so who buys more shoes ... men or women?"

The audience will instantly respond with, "Oh, women do! Women buy a lot more shoes than men!"

I will then poll the audience and ask the men how many pairs of shoes they own. I will typically get answers that range from two pairs to maybe 25.

However, when I ask the women in the audience how many pairs of shoes they own, I will typically get answers that run as high as 50, 100, and maybe even more than 200 pairs.

Of course, I will also get answers that are outside the norm. I will get some men with 50 pairs of shoes and more. I also get women who own only four to ten pairs of shoes.

Yes, this is a real difference across 325 million Americans. If you ever go to a store with a shoe department, you will typically see that the women's shoe department is three or four times larger than the men's.

However, this real difference becomes an insulting stereotype if I go up to an individual woman and say, "Oh, you're a woman. I'll bet you really like shoes, huh?"

Why is this insulting? Because it is now a stereotype. If I take this real difference that is statistically true across the population and then apply that real difference to one individual woman, then I am labeling her. I am assuming I know something about her as an individual based on a statistical likelihood. In other words, I cannot apply a real difference based on a statistical calculation to an individual. I have to consider that person for whom he or she is in reality ... which means:

> **I actually have to get to know you!**

But then, I don't want to do that. Getting to know another person is a lot of work. It is much easier to just stick a label on you.

It is amazing how often we have problems distinguishing between real differences and stereotypes. I run into this all the time from people who cannot wait to be offended. Their brains are primed to be offended over anything that even mentions the fact that we might be different from one another. Again, it is as if they have this "Mission from God" syndrome where they want to smite anyone who ever says anything that identifies someone by their race, religion, gender, age, and so on. It has been explained to me that making such references is offensive because it is gender, age, or religion specific, to mention a few. However, such a view of the world is simply not reality. There are many differences that truly do exist between us, and I think that is a good thing. Isn't that what diversity is all about? To ignore the fact that there are differences between us is to ignore diversity itself.

I recently had this experience with a group of younger people who were very offended over a gender specific reference I made in one of my sessions.

In this session, I explained that 5,000 years ago we were all food. If we were attacked by a bear or a lion, and if we did not have any type of weapon on hand, we really didn't have any way to defend ourselves. I mean, what are you going to do to the lion? Bite it? Could you claw it?

I then said, "Even those ladies with the press-on nails are not going to do much damage to that lion."

Now, no one said anything during the session. Instead, once it was all over, they ran to the owner to complain. I had made a gender specific reference to women and that was horribly offensive, apparently. Their argument was that I was stereotyping all women as wearing fake nails, even though some men wear them as well. It was the *Hang 'Em High* approach to conflict resolution all over again.

Of course, this passive aggressive attack did not seem to bother anyone at the organization. That is how they always handle their conflicts. Unfortunately, that was why I was called into present to them in the first place. It was not safe to disagree with anyone there. There was no trust at all, so the environment was toxic.

When I spoke to the owner later, who just happened to be one of the worst enablers I have ever met, he explained why the employees were so upset.

"You made a gender specific reference about women wearing press-on nails. That is what offended them," he told me.

"But why is that offensive?" I asked the owner.

"Because you singled out the women," he told me.

"OK, but who wears fake nails more often, men or women?" I asked.

The owner replied, "There are some men who wear fake nails, you know."

"Yes, I know what you are saying. But across 325 million Americans, who wears fake nails more in this country, men or women?" I asked.

"I guess women do," the owner said.

"Of course, they do. That is a fact and it is a real difference between men and women. Just go to any nail salon in this country and you will see who makes up their clientele. I did not apply this statement to any single person. I did not point anyone out and say that they must wear press-on nails because they are female, which would have been a stereotype. But this is a real difference that truly does exist. It sounds to me like they are upset because I pointed out a statistical difference that really does exist between most men and women, right?" I asked.

"Yes, but it is offensive today to make a gender specific reference," he told me.

"But does that really make sense? We say we value diversity, but anytime we make a factual reference to any of the real differences that truly do exist between us, differences we are all supposed to appreciate, that is somehow offensive? Are we supposed to just live in a world that ignores reality? Again, I did not apply this difference to any individual. I mentioned it as a real difference that exists across most people, and that is a fact. In order for me to know if one of your female employees wears press-on nails, I would have to get to know her. I cannot just assume she does because she is female. That would be taking a real difference across millions of people and turning it into a stereotype. That truly would be offensive," I said.

This is the same thing as referring to women wearing makeup, lipstick, and dresses. Do some men wear makeup, lipstick, and dresses? Yes, some do. But across 325 million Americans, isn't that a real difference between us? Of course, it would become a stereotype if I applied this real difference to an individual woman by just assuming she presented herself in that way.

Unfortunately, that is exactly what is happening in every part of society today, and it is causing us to inadvertently offend each other, which in turn gives us the good old *Hang 'Em High* mentality that is killing us all. But then, too many people today can't wait to attack someone for maybe saying the wrong thing just so they show everyone that they are the sole defender of right and wrong in the world. (Again, insert much sarcasm here.)

In one of my D&I presentations, we somehow got on the topic of Black players in the NBA and in college. I then mentioned that it is not easy for most of us to name great NBA players who are White. Most are Black.

One woman, who was White, by the way, yelled out to me that what I said was very offensive. Apparently, I was being "race specific."

When I asked what she meant by me being "race specific," she told me I was singling out someone by their race, and that is really offensive.

Of course, I admired her more for calling me out than the passive aggressive Retreaters who were possibly sitting in the audience and planning to stab me in the back later. These Retreaters would have never given me a chance to respond to the accusation. That is why the passive aggressive Retreaters are far worse than the Attackers, although neither one will have many happy relationships in their lives. If you cannot address and resolve conflicts in your life, GAME OVER.

So, I turned to the audience and asked, "Maybe she has a point. Is it a stereotype to say that most of the players in college basketball and the NBA are Black?"

As soon as this question passed my lips, the audience instantly shouted, "They are Black."

I then asked, "OK, so name some of the great basketball players in the NBA right now who are Black."

Instantly, several names shot out, like Lebron James, James Harden, Anthony Davis, and Stephen Curry, to mention a few. There were more names given to me than I could write on the large post-it note hanging in the front of the room.

I then asked them to give me some names of great basketball players in the NBA who are White. The room grew silent.

Then, someone threw out, "Larry Bird."

"Yes," I responded. "But Larry is retired. He's a hall of famer now. Can anyone think of any current NBA players who are White?"

Everyone thought for a minute, then someone shouted, "Kevin Love."

"Yes," I responded. "Kevin Love. He's a great player with the Cavs. Anyone else?"

Everyone thought for another few seconds. Someone then called out, "Kevin Love."

"Yes, but we already said Kevin Love. Anyone else?" I asked.

"There's that Luca guy from the Mavs," someone else called out.

"What is his last name?" I asked.

"I don't know. Most of these guys are from those eastern bloc countries. I can't pronounce any of their names. It's a lot like hockey!" he answered.

Someone else yelled out, "Kyle Kuzma."

"Kyle Kuzma is Black, you idiot," someone replied.

"No, he's not. Look at his nose. It's like he's Italian, or maybe Jewish, or something. But he's as White as me," the man replied.

By then, everyone was Googling to find White basketball players.

Another person yelled out, "Oh! Tyler Johnson. He's with Brooklyn."

"He's African American, too," a Black man replied.

"No, he's not. I've got a pic of him right here. See," the man replied, showing everyone his phone.

"He looks Amish. What's with the beard?" A woman chimed in. "He's also missing a tooth. You would think he could afford to get that fixed."

And on and on it went.

I then asked the attendees, "Is there a real difference in the NBA regarding the number of White players and Black players?"

I then heard a strong, "Yes" from most of the attendees, as many laughed at the obvious difference.

"Is that a stereotype?" I asked.

"No," I heard from the audience.

"Then aren't there some things in this world that might be race specific because it is true?" I asked.

The audience agreed.

We then agreed that recognizing the truth is not a bad thing if it is true, including the woman who was originally offended by what I said. She had just never thought of it that way. But then, that is why you go to seminars and read books like this, isn't it? Don't you want to get someone else's viewpoint?

"So, does that mean I can just go up to a person who is Black and assume they can play basketball, like Stanley Hudson from *The Office* or Chris Rock from *Everybody Hates Chris*?" I asked. (If you don't get these references, just Google *The Office* basketball and *Everybody Hates Chris* basketball. It is worth your time to see these stereotypes in action. Simply asking Chris Rock and Stanley Hudson if they could play would have saved a lot of grief ... but it wouldn't have been as funny.)

The audience laughed at these references and I heard an enthusiastic, "No!"

"Then how would I ever know if someone is a good basketball player or bad one?" I asked.

"You have to talk to them!" I heard back.

Their responses summed up my point about real differences and stereotypes perfectly. Unfortunately, not only is the human brain predisposed to go right into fight or flight, but it is also wired to stereotype everything we see.

Stereotyping and the Human Brain

In order to process the billions of pieces of information our brain must store and retrieve, it is actually wired to simplify things. This is why we humans naturally put things into categories. We do this with everything, such as animals, food, movies, and so on. For each category we assign to an object, we will also develop an entire script to go with it. We will organize and group things together like, "These fruits are good because they are sweet, but these are not. These vegetables are good, but these make me sick. These animals are cute, but these will eat me," and so on.

When we do this with people, we call this stereotyping, and all humans do it. It is a universal trait amongst humans.[193]

With people, we might categorize them according to their athletic ability, intelligence, honesty, and so on. These various labels we assign to different people can become so ingrained in our brains that within 17,000ths of a second our subconscious can kick in and instantly affect the way we treat this person and how we make decisions, especially when we were primed with this information in our first three years of life.

For example, simply seeing an older Asian female can generate many different beliefs, like she is smart, she's a bad driver, she has a certain accent, she is probably wealthy, and she must eat a lot of rice and vegetables. Again, whenever we make these associations, we call that bias. Again, this can all happen in 17,000ths of a second, faster than you can blink.[194]

When we categorize other people according to what our culture tells us is true, it all seems reasonable to us based on our personal experiences and what everyone around us tells us. Our brain doesn't group people together to harm us. Quite to the contrary. It is trying to protect us by simplifying a very confusing and complex world for us to better understand. That is why all humans do this, not just the evil ones. If our brains did not do this, they would become overloaded with the tremendous amount of information thrown at them every day. Again, we are all operating with a 5,000-year-old brain. In Fred Flintstone's time, properly categorizing the world could easily mean the difference between life and death.[195]

Can You Recognize Other Faces?

One of the fastest ways to see if you hold biases towards other people is to see if you can recognize the faces of others who are a different race than you. If not, don't be upset. All that means is that you are human and you need to work harder at it.

Scientists have known for decades that humans are simply better at recognizing the faces of their own race than the faces of other races. This is now called the "other race effect." The other race effect is a universal phenomenon that cuts across all racial groups in countries all over the world.[196]

Learning how to recognize faces of your own race starts when we are infants and it only gets stronger over time. By the time babies are only three months old, their brains react more strongly to faces of their own race than to faces of people who look different from them. Again, this race-selective response only grows stronger as children grow older, which suggests it is driven, in part, by the circumstances of our lives.[197]

If you think of this phenomenon from Fred Flintstone's perspective, it makes perfect sense. Fred would very likely go through his entire life without ever seeing anyone who looked different from him. To Fred, it was important to recognize people of his own race, but not of other races. If Fred ever ran into someone who looked different from him, that could mean he was in potential danger. It could mean that Fred's territory was being invaded. This is how Fred could distinguish friends from foes. Now, just because someone looked different from Fred did not mean they posed any threat to him. But if you lived in a time of such tenuous survival as Fred, did you want to take that chance? We humans just naturally learn to better recognize faces of our own race, or the people we see the most as we develop into adults.

For years, we have always classified someone as a bigot whenever we hear the famous phrase, "Hey, they all look alike to me." However, this is true of all of us. Due to biology and exposure, our brains are simply better at recognizing faces that are more familiar to us.[198] This simply means that we all have biases living in our brains. This, of course, isn't permission for anyone to go around acting on these biases. Instead, we must all be aware of what is living in our subconscious brains, and then work to overcome these biases. And yes, it will not be easy. We humans certainly have our work cut out for us.

Interestingly, children who are adopted by parents of another race do not typically exhibit the other race effect. Researchers in Belgium found that Chinese and Vietnamese children who were adopted by White families were just as good at recognizing White faces as they were at recognizing Asian faces.[199]

This is because the brain is not really a hardwired machine. As we already discussed, the brain will physically conform itself to the environment and experiences we subject it to every day. Again, this is called neuroplasticity.[200]

Recognizing faces is an extremely complicated neurological process. For us to recognize other faces and their many expressions, multiple areas of the brain must be engaged simultaneously.[201]

The Purse Snatchers

In her book, *BIASED*, Dr. Jennifer Eberhardt, tells the story of how the Chinatown shopping district in Oakland, California was being targeted by a group of purse snatchers back in 2014. Apparently, some Black teenagers were roaming the streets of Chinatown, targeting older Asian women and then snatching their purses away from them. Yes, they were mugging the little old Asian ladies.[202]

The police would make arrests, but the cases against the Black teens would quickly fall apart when the older Chinese women could not identify the purse snatcher from a police lineup. Even though the Black teens did not wear masks and the Asian ladies clearly saw their faces, none of the Asian women could identify their muggers.[203]

Interestingly, the Black teens never wore masks and they always targeted the older Chinese ladies because they knew the Asian women couldn't tell them apart from each other anyway. Their naturally Black face was the perfect disguise.[204]

After the city put cameras in the streets of Chinatown, the game was up. Once the teens were arrested, they were asked why they targeted these particular women. The Black teens freely admitted, "The Asian people can't ID. They just can't tell the brothers apart."[205]

Of course, the teens did not target the Black ladies they saw walking around in Chinatown. Why? Because the older Black ladies could recognize them and later identify the Black teens even if they got just a quick glance at them. They were used to recognizing Black faces.[206]

Overcoming Stereotypes

Whenever I think of our inability to recognize the faces of other races, I always think of Steve Irwin, The Crocodile Hunter. I remember seeing his show on several occasions and he could always tell his crocodiles apart from one another. To me, they all looked alike, and they all looked evil. I was afraid of them, for obvious reasons.

However, Irwin could not only identify each crocodile by name, but he would also describe them as being "real beauties." To me, there was not a beautiful one in the bunch. They all looked like Satan and they all wanted to eat me.

I noticed as I watched his show more and more, I could start to see what he was talking about. I became more familiar with their different markings, sizes and structures. After a while, I could actually begin to tell a crocodile apart from an alligator. I never did get to the point where I thought any of them were beautiful, but as I learned more about them, I could start to tell them apart. Neurologically, that makes sense because crocodiles are not just another race from me, but they are a completely different species.

Again, that is how the human brain can rewire itself. We can overcome the priming we all received as children that is filled with stereotypes and myths. You have to learn more about other people and build up your familiarity. If not, you will one day fall victim to the implicit biases that live in your brain, and that will be bad for you. It is a matter of exposing your brain to the right information.

Do We See Black People as Being Dangerous?

Clearly, our brains are wired to detect any potential threats in 17,000ths of a second, which puts us into an instant state of fight or flight. As we have discussed, there have been several studies that clearly show that most of us perceive African Americans as posing a threat, and that applies to both White and Black people alike. Unfortunately, that is how most of us have been primed.

To accurately gauge the level of threat someone might pose to us, we humans must also be able to accurately assess the physical size and strength of others. Of course, this then begs the question, "If we see Blacks as being more dangerous than others, would we then also perceive Blacks as being bigger and stronger than they really are, which would make them appear to pose more of a threat?" Since little research had been conducted addressing this issue, researchers John Paul Wilson, Kurt Hugenberg, and Nicholas Rule decided to investigate.[207]

These researchers conducted a series of experiments where hundreds of participants from across the United States were shown a series of color photographs of White and Black male faces who were all of equal height and weight. The participants were then asked to estimate the height, weight, strength, and overall muscular structure of the men they were shown.[208]

"We found that these estimates were consistently biased. Participants judged the Black men to be larger, stronger, and more muscular than the White men, even though they were actually the same size," said Dr. Wilson of Montclair State University. "Participants also believed that the Black men were more capable of causing harm in a hypothetical altercation and that the police would be more justified in using force to subdue them, even if the men were unarmed," Wilson said.[209]

In one of the experiments, the participants were shown Black and White bodies that were identical in size and strength. However, the participants were still more likely to view the Black males as being taller and heavier than their White male counterparts.[210]

In another experiment, the size bias was most pronounced for the men who had facial features more associated with Blacks than with Whites.[211]

"We found that men with darker skin and more stereotypically Black facial features tended to most likely elicit biased size perceptions, even though they were actually no larger than men with lighter skin and less stereotypical facial features," said Wilson. "Thus, the size bias doesn't rely just on a White versus Black group boundary. It also varies within Black men according to their facial features."[212]

Wilson said that one reason Black men are disproportionately more likely to be killed in interactions with police, even when they are unarmed, is because police officers are likely to misperceive their size and strength. This could contribute to police officers' decisions to shoot.[213]

This is all the more reason to recognize and overcome the biases in our subconscious.

Myths

Unfortunately, we need to take some time and address the many myths that circulate throughout our society.

Myths about other people have been around for centuries. These myths typically get started because someone wants to dehumanize another group. So, we conjure up some fantastic lie, spread it to as many people as we can, and, eventually, people believe it.

According to one of the greatest spin masters of all time: "If you tell a lie long enough, it becomes the truth."

That was said by Joseph Goebbels, the Reich Minister of Propaganda of Nazi Germany from 1933 to 1945.

Would *Intelligent* People Be Betrayed by Their Subconscious Bigotry?

Bigotry is not an issue of IQ. It is an issue of Emotional Quotient, or EQ. You can be a highly educated person and still be an emotional child who is intolerant of anyone who disagrees with you. Actually, the smarter you are and the more successful you become, the chances of you engaging in confirmation bias actually skyrockets. Why? Because your ego cannot take being wrong, which explains NASA and the space shuttle disasters.

> **Yes, far too many people don't let the facts get in the way of a good opinion.**

For instance, I have heard for years that the nerve endings in Black people are not as sensitive as those found in White, Asian, or Hispanic people. I have also heard that Black people's skin is thicker than White people's, so Blacks do not feel pain the same way as White people do. These myths go all the way back to the days of slavery when slave masters would beat their slaves and subject them to horrendous physical conditions. How do you justify mistreating another human being like that? You just make something up, like, "They just don't feel pain like we do."[214]

(I hope you recognize the obvious dehumanization going on here.)

Not only did many of the average people believe these myths back in the 1800's, but so did some of the top medical experts in the country. Dr. J. Marion Sims, the celebrated father of modern gynecology, took Black female slaves and conducted live medical experiments on them without using any form of anesthesia. From 1845 to 1849, Dr. Sims practiced some of the most painful operations imaginable on the enslaved women of Alabama from his office in Montgomery. In his autobiography, *The Story of My Life,* Sims described in detail the horrendous agony these Black women suffered as he surgically cut into their genitals again and again in an attempt to perfect his surgical techniques to repair some of the severe complications women can suffer from an obstructed childbirth.[215]

Yes, the infamous Nazi, Dr. Josef Mengele, had nothing on Dr. Sims.

It is easy to hear these myths and dismiss them as a sign of the times. I mean, these myths started well over 250 years ago and modern science back then was not what it is today. Clearly, no educated person would still believe these myths now? Right? Guess again.

In a 2016 study, researchers discovered that still today at least half of White medical students and residents believe at least one myth about these physiological differences between Blacks and Whites, including that Black people's nerve endings are less sensitive than Whites. When White medical students and residents were asked to imagine how much pain White or Black patients would experience in various hypothetical situations, the medical students and residents insisted that Black people felt less pain. As a result, Black Americans today are systematically undertreated for pain in relation to their White counterparts. Further research has shown that when compared to White patients, Black patients are less likely to be given pain medications at all, and, if they are given pain medication, they receive lower quantities.[216]

Recent data also shows that present day doctors fail to sufficiently treat the pain of Black adults and children for many medical issues. In a 2013 review of various studies examining racial disparities in pain management, which was published in *The American Medical Association Journal of Ethics*, researchers found that Black and Hispanic people, which ranged from children who needed tonsillectomies to elders who were placed into hospice care, received inadequate pain management compared to their White counterparts.[217]

How could this happen? I mean, this is the 21st century. Physicians are some of the most highly educated and respected professionals in our society today. Would educated people actually believe these myths? Of course, they would. They are human and some of them were primed to believe these myths since they were born.

This is why it is important to learn about our history and debunk these myths that are still passed onto our children today. Myths, just like bigotry and racism, die when they are exposed to the light.

We must never think that we are too smart or sophisticated to fall victim to these ridiculous myths. But remember, these myths are very different from the stereotypes we just discussed. With stereotypes, there might be a real difference between us when you consider the entire population from a statistical standpoint, such as who buys more shoes, men or women? Just because something might be statistically true, that does not mean I can apply that statistical difference to someone as an individual. Instead, I must get to know you.

A myth, on the other hand, was never true. It was most likely developed as part of a dehumanization process designed to oppress someone else or to justify something evil we wanted to do to someone.

Again, it is important to slow down and think before we make decisions and to actually examine the facts before we make up our minds. We all need to start doing that more often.

Are There Myths and Stereotypes About Police Officers?

Years ago, a cousin of mine, Chris Claypool, was a police officer in Ohio with the Columbus Police Department. Chris was everything you wanted in a police officer. His level of emotional intelligence and self-control were off the charts. He could calm any situation. He truly was the perfect cop.

Chris was actually a gentle giant. He was about 6' 3" tall and well built. He was an imposing figure. However, his controlled demeanor and kind face was what got your attention. You could not have met Chris without walking away impressed.

Chris was actually so impressive that he quickly rose up through the ranks of the Columbus Police Department and was promoted to the rank of lieutenant. I had no doubt that one day Chris would be the Chief of Police for the city of Columbus. That would be a great day for all of us.

Soon after he was promoted to the rank of lieutenant, he was driving into work late one Saturday night when a call came in about a stranded motorist on Refugee Road. Chris radioed in and said he would take the call since it was right on his way into work. Of course, being a police lieutenant, he did not have to take the call. However, that was Chris being Chris.

As Chris got out of his police cruiser, a car suddenly came out of nowhere, sped up, and ran him down. A witness said the driver was clearly targeting him. Chris was killed by a lone coward hiding behind the wheel of a car.

The news devastated the entire family. Chris' wife, Tammy, was completely overcome with shock and grief. It was as if she had been run over as well. She was inconsolable. I have never seen anyone racked with so much grieving pain in my life, and I still haven't.

Chris was a true human being, a husband, a father, and a friend, but to the person who ran him down, I know Chris was just another cop. A pig.

The misconceptions this motorist had about Chris were all either myths or stereotypes. Are there bad cops who never should have been given a badge? Yes. Are there still cops out there who should lose their badges? Absolutely.

Today, Chris would be more upset than anyone with the bad cops who reinforce these myths and stereotypes placed upon police officers everywhere. He would have been the perfect advocate for reforming law enforcement everywhere because he was the role model everyone should follow. He could have been the national symbol of what it means to protect and serve. As our world becomes more chaotic, all I think of is, "What if ... ?"

In the recent riots that occurred in 2020 over George Floyd's killing, I thought of Chris every day. Astonishingly, we also had riots here in Columbus, Ohio. This does not happen in Columbus. We get upset, but we don't riot. We still have cows that get out onto our highways. We are a big town. We do not riot and cause tens of millions of dollars in property damage. However, all of this happened just a few short miles from my house.

During the riots, a video surfaced of a White man giving African Americans money to riot and to destroy property in the downtown area. Of course, we don't know if he had any political affiliations. Everything about the man's motives is pure speculation. However, the harm he incited is clear: Fight fire with fire and ignore the teachings of Thoreau, Gandhi, Martin Luther King, Jr., John Lewis, and Lt. Chris Claypool.[218]

After the riots were over, downtown was spray painted with all kinds of derogatory insults against the police, like "F" the police, and so on. I am sure the people who wrote that did not see the bigotry in what they were doing. But what if someone spray painted "F- the Blacks," or "F the Jews" or "F the gays"? We would all instantly recognize the bigotry.

What is the difference between grouping all police officers together and grouping all Blacks together? All Jews? All Muslims? And so on? Nothing.

> **Bigotry is a universal human trait.
> However, we only tend to see it
> when others do it to us.**

Everybody loses when we label each other and attack each other based on these misperceptions. Again, whatever we do to others will eventually boomerang back to us. Maybe, just maybe, as a national calling, we can stop, think and ask ourselves, "What would Chris do?"

"I'm just different. That's all."

Elijah McClain was a 23-year-old African American massage therapist living in Aurora, Colorado in 2019.[219]

In his free time, Elijah volunteered at an animal shelter to play his violin for the cats because he thought they were lonely. Friends said that his gentleness with animals extended to humans as well. One of his clients recalled him as being "the sweetest, purest person I have ever met. He was definitely a light in a whole lot of darkness." Another acquaintance said, "I don't even think he would set a mouse trap if there was a rodent problem."[220]

Elijah had never been arrested or charged with a crime in his life. His friends and family described him as a "spiritual seeker, pacifist, oddball, vegetarian, athlete, and peacemaker who was exceedingly gentle."[221]

However, on August 24, 2019, just after 10:30 pm, Elijah was walking home from a convenience store close to his home. He was wearing a ski mask as he often did to keep his face warm because of an underlying blood condition. Elijah was not only anemic, but it was also in the mid-60s that night. To Elijah, it was cold outside.[222]

It is also believed that Elijah was autistic. So, he may have also been wearing a ski-mask to calm himself due to his autism disorder.[223]

However, a neighbor who saw Elijah walking home called 911. The caller said Elijah was acting suspicious because he was dancing, wearing a ski mask, and listening to music on his way home. However, the same caller confirmed that Elijah was unarmed and that he didn't think he or anyone else was in danger.[224]

Elijah had not committed any crime and was not doing anything illegal.[225]

Three Aurora police officers arrived, Nathan Woodyard, Jason Rosenblatt, and Randy Roedema. One officer can be heard in the body cam recording admitting that Elijah had not done anything illegal. They then questioned him, detained him, and placed him under arrest without telling him what crime he committed. As the arrest was happening, Elijah became understandably more agitated, which I can tell you from my own personal life experience, is a really bad thing for most people with autism. Many people with autism do not like to be touched because many of their senses, including their sense of touch, can be greatly amplified. He asked the officers to, "Please respect my boundaries."[226]

During this process, all three of the officers either shut off, tampered with, or altered the positions of their body cameras so no one could see what they were doing to Elijah. However, the audio recording portion of the body cam came through loud and clear, which gives us excellent insight as to what really happened.

As they started to arrest Elijah, you can hear him pleading with the police to stop, explaining he was "stopping [his] music to listen."[227]

The officers held him on the ground in a carotid control hold, which restricts blood flow to the brain from the carotid arteries, for 15 minutes. Elijah can be heard telling the officers he hadn't done anything wrong and that he couldn't breathe, a plea we have heard way too many times before.[228]

You can hear him throughout the recording sobbing, apologizing for vomiting after the police choked him, telling them he doesn't like being touched and is an introvert, and telling them he loves them.[229]

Some of Elijah's last words can be heard in the audio recordings.

"I can't breathe. I have my ID right here ..."

"My name is Elijah McClain. That's my house. I was just going home. I'm an introvert..."

"I'm just different. That's all. I'm so sorry. I have no gun. I don't do that stuff. I don't do any fighting. Why are you attacking me? I don't even kill flies. I don't eat meat."

"But I don't judge people, I don't judge people who do eat meat. Forgive me. All I was trying to do was become better... I will do it... I will do anything..."

"Try to forgive me. I'm a mood Gemini. I'm sorry. I'm so sorry. Ow, that really hurt."[230]

Candace Bailey, a civil rights advocate in Aurora, said, "Anyone who listens to the audio of Elijah McClain dying ends up crying. And if you do not, you are part of the problem."[231]

Elijah then vomited and said, "I wasn't trying to do that. I just can't breathe correctly."[232]

As Elijah continued to uncontrollably vomit, an officer threatens him, saying: "If you keep messing around, I'm going to bring my dog out, and he's going to bite you, you understand me?"[233]

These desperate pleas from Elijah went unheeded not only by the three officers who first responded to the 911 call, but also by the others who arrived on the scene later. They can be heard chatting casually as Elijah struggled for his last few breaths.[234]

In these audio recordings, you can also hear one officer saying he was "acting crazy," that he was "definitely on something," and that he attacked them with "incredible, crazy strength." At one point, all three officers were on top of him.[235]

When the paramedics arrived on the scene, Elijah was already handcuffed and restrained on the ground.[236] One medic estimated Elijah's weight to be about 220 pounds, which is about 110 kilograms. The medic gave him an injection of 500 mg of ketamine, which is a powerful sedative. However, the standard dose of ketamine is 5 milligrams per each kilogram of a person's weight. The coroner's report states that Elijah's height was actually about 5 feet 6 inches tall and he only weighed about 140 pounds, or 64 kilograms. That meant Elijah should have received a dosage of about 320 milligrams, *not* 500, which is almost 60% more than he should have been given.[237]

Elijah went into cardiac arrest on the way to the hospital.[238] He died in the hospital a couple days later on August 30, 2019. His family said he was brain dead and covered in bruises.[239]

The case of Elijah McClain is a complete tragedy and demonstrates every kind of prejudice and bias we have been discussing:

- Elijah was Black, so research would suggest that his actions were seen as being more violent than if he was White.

- Elijah was also autistic, which could easily explain why he was acting the way he was and why he reacted to the police the way he did when they tried to restrain him.

- The paramedic gave Elijah an overdose of ketamine that was 60% more than his body weight could handle. Since most people see Black males as being larger and stronger than they really are, the paramedic estimated Elijah's weight to be about 220 pounds when he was only about 140.

- In the audio recordings, you can hear the other officers saying he was acting crazy, that he was definitely on something, and that he had attacked them with incredible, crazy strength, when Elijah was not under the influence of anything. He had a disability. He was autistic. He did not have incredible, crazy strength. He was just Black.

We as a society must demand reform for not just the police and paramedics of the world, but for all of us. Otherwise, I do not believe we or our civilization will survive.

God help you if you live in America and you are different ... in any way.

We truly need the Chris Claypool's of the world right now more than ever.

8

SKILL # 5: DON'T BE AN ENABLER!

This final skill might be the most difficult for people because it relies so heavily on our emotional intelligence and it flies right in the face of what many of us consider to be "nice." However, this last skill is absolutely vital if we are ever going to see a positive change in our workplaces and in the world.

Most people consider themselves to be nice. They get up every day, they go to work, they would never burn a cross on someone's lawn, and they go about their days trying not to harm others. However, we are all human, which means, once again, we are usually run by our primitive fight or flight response.

Since most of us think of ourselves as good decent people, we do not like conflict. That means most people would rather avoid a conflict than engage. To avoid an issue, most of us move into passive aggressive mode. We become Retreaters. If you are like most people, you will smile to my face, make me think everything is fine, and then stab me in the back when I am not looking. Of course, we rationalize this destructive behavior by saying we are just being nice. However, that is not being nice. It is just another form of evil.

Retreaters are the worst communicators on the planet. They suppress their conflicts for the moment, only to engage in terrorist, behind-your-back tactics later. Retreaters break the one cardinal rule for all organizations to be successful: They kill the trust.

Retreaters prove to everyone that it is not safe to disagree with them. They prove to everyone that they will "get" anyone who disagrees with them. They prove it is not safe.

Enabling is Evil

Martin Luther King, Jr. might have put it best:

> **"There comes a time
> when silence is betrayal."**

That is what passive aggressives, or Retreaters, do. Their silence only encourages the bully's current behavior to continue by giving it tacit approval.

In fact, wherever there is bullying, you will find Retreaters at work. We expect evil people to be evil, such as in the case of Enron, Nazi Germany, the genocide of the Armenians and, of course, the great epidemic of bullying currently going on in our workplaces and schools.

None of this bullying would continue without enablers. That is why we have so much bullying in our world, even though there are many more good people than bad ones. But if there are so many more good people than bad ones, then why do we have a world that is full of bullying? It is because most of us are Retreaters and we let it happen.

In fact, bullies do not want your help when they are bullying others. They actually don't need your help. All they need from you is to step aside and not interfere. That is complicit enough.

That is why the EEOC included in its 2016 *Select Task Force on the Study of Harassment in the Workplace* report that bystander intervention should now be included in every organization's training.

Bystander intervention has been shown to be especially effective in preventing unwelcome and harassing behavior.[240] In fact, studies show that when a bystander speaks up, the harassing behavior ends within 10 seconds 57% of the time.[241]

Bystander intervention training is effective because:

- It creates awareness by educating bystanders to recognize potentially problematic behaviors when they see them.
- It creates a sense of collective responsibility, which motivates bystanders to step in and take action when they see problematic behavior.
- It creates a sense of empowerment in most people by educating potential bystanders in how to properly address and resolve conflict, which includes using their EPR skills.
- It educates bystanders by teaching them who they should contact to get help with a situation.[242]

According to the EEOC, a totally new approach to designing and conducting this training is needed, and I adamantly agree.

Think of every scandal you have ever seen and you will also see a whole crowd of nice people watching it all happen, doing everything they can to enable the villain. However, overcoming our natural tendency to become Retreaters whenever conflict arises takes a great deal of courage, which, again, takes a high level of emotional intelligence.

The Evil Enablers

Would you disagree with a superior if you thought they were about to seriously injure or kill someone? Would you stand by and let something like that happen because your boss is a powerful person or an expert in their field? Would you speak up if you thought it would get you into trouble at work or maybe even get you fired?

Don't answer too quickly if you are human.

In 1961, Nazi war criminal Adolf Eichmann went on trial for the role he played in the Holocaust. With the Holocaust and Eichmann in mind, Yale University psychologist Stanley Milgram devised an experiment to help explain why millions of people supported the Nazi's in committing such horrendous crimes. In addressing this issue, Milgram posed the following question: "Could it be that Eichmann and his million accomplices in the Holocaust really were just following orders?"[243]

This famous study has become known as the "Milgram Experiment."

In answering this question, Milgram conducted a series of social psychology experiments designed to determine if people would follow the directives of an authority figure even if it caused harm to others. The participants in the study were men who came from many different occupations with varying levels of education. In these experiments, the participants were told they were actually assisting with another study, but they had to administer electric shocks to a learner, who was not in the room, in order to conduct the experiment. Even though the participants could not see the learner, they could hear the learner shout in pain from the shocks they were inflicting on him. Of course, the learner was not a real person. It was a recording of someone yelling out in pain, but the participants didn't know that.[244]

In the experiment, the authority figure simply instructed the participants to deliver increasingly higher levels of electric shock. The participants were instructed to continue delivering these electric shocks, even though these shocks gradually increased to the point where they would have been fatal if the learner had been a real person.[245]

Amazingly, Milgram found that many of the participants actually followed the directives they were given, even when it came to delivering deadly levels of electricity to the learner, although some of them did it reluctantly.[246]

The experiment has been repeated several times around the world with many different subjects, but the results have all been fairly consistent.[247]

According to the Milgram Experiment, people will often follow the directives of an authority figure even if it causes harm to others.

So, what would you do? Would you commit illegal or immoral acts if you were told to and if it was part of your job? Well, consider this situation. In 2019, Dr. William Husel, an intensive care doctor with Mount Carmel West Hospital in Columbus, Ohio, was charged with 25 counts of murder for prescribing critically ill patients fatal doses of fentanyl.[248]

Fentanyl is one of the most powerful opioids ever developed. It is 50 to 100 times more powerful than morphine. Even very small doses can be fatal.[249]

The prosecutor leading the case against Husel said investigators only focused on cases where Dr. Husel administered doses of 500 to 2,000 micrograms of fentanyl to patients.[250]

Just so you will understand how high these doses were, a typical dose of fentanyl could be up to 100 micrograms for patients, depending on their size and the circumstances of their condition. However, Husel ordered these patients to be injected with anywhere from five to twenty times the maximum dosage that is typically allowed.[251]

Dr. Lewis Nelson, a professor of emergency medicine at Rutgers New Jersey Medical School and an expert on opioid prescriptions said, "These are very high fentanyl doses for patients without significant opioid tolerance." He went onto say that 2,000 micrograms of fentanyl, or even 500 micrograms, "would generally prove consequential and most likely lethal" in most patients.[252]

However, the main point here is that Husel could not have acted alone in administering these lethal doses of fentanyl. These dosages had to be approved by a pharmacist and were then typically administered by the nurses.[253]

Since Dr. Husel was also certified in anesthesiology, his credentials gave him great authority. The prosecutor said that whenever a nurse questioned him, he was able to give some type of reasonable explanation for what he was doing. As a result, the nurses at Mount Carmel, some of whom were newly hired, went ahead and administered these lethal doses.[254]

During the investigation, dozens of nurses, pharmacists and managers were put on administrative leave. Several of these employees could also face further action from agencies like the Ohio Board of Nursing. "It could not have happened without some complicit knowledge among nurses, pharmacists and supervisors," said Gerry Leeseberg, a lawyer who represents the families suing the hospital.[255]

One former Mount Carmel nurse said Husel was generally respected and popular. However, she heard other doctors complaining about the high dosages Husel was ordering, but nothing was ever done. This nurse claimed that she and other nurses also complained to the leaders of their units about these

SKILL # 5: DON'T BE AN ENABLER!

high dosages, but nothing ever seemed to be done about their complaints.[256]

One of the lawyers representing some of the patients' families was much more direct. She said if a doctor ordered doses of 1,000 micrograms or more of fentanyl, "I would think 'Have you lost your mind?' Did you mistype a zero? I wouldn't ever give it, because I know I'd kill them."[257]

So, how could all of this happen? Why did so many trained professionals, doctors, nurses, and pharmacists alike not speak up when Dr. Husel was overdosing patients?

Well, that is easy. Hospitals typically foster a culture where bullying, intolerant, bigoted, emotional children can thrive, so the enablers never said a word. In many hospitals, the initials M.D. really means "Minor Deity." If you disagree with a physician, you take your professional life into your hands.

This is the same reason why only a few people spoke up at NASA before 14 astronauts were blown out of the sky. It is also why Dr. Larry Nassar was able to molest so many USA female gymnasts across a 14-year period. It is why Penn State University settled a child rape case on behalf of Jerry Sandusky in 1971, and then actively covered it up and enabled him to continue molesting little boys until he was finally caught again in 2011 by the Patriot News. Bullying, intolerant, bigoted, emotional children were running these organizations, so it was not safe to speak up. Whenever it is not safe to speak up, trust dies and the enablers populate like rabbits.[258]

The world is full of enablers. Enablers will follow the evil orders of an authority figure and rationalize away the consequences of what they are doing. The old defense, "Hey, I was just doing my job" is still alive and well in the world because humans are still running things. Since we are all human, most of us would rather be Retreaters, or passive aggressive, and ignore the problem, even when it involves murder. It is easier to just go along than cause any problems or disrupt the status quo.

> **In the end, we all become enablers when we remain silent.**

Of course, this also takes us back to the beginning of this book. There is only one question we will ever need to ask to assess the culture of these organizations:

Is It Safe?

Is it safe to speak up? If not, there is no trust and we are all doomed.

The scourge of my existence are the people I meet who are passive aggressive Retreaters. They will simply not stand up for what is right. They watch other people get bullied all day long, and they do nothing. They see injustice happen, and they turn away. This means disaster will surely strike the organization one day, as well as for themselves.

Enablers always end up on the "Naughty List."

And don't even get me started on most lawyers, or more correctly, I should say most litigators. Yes, it is a lawyer's job to defend their clients. However, don't ever think that because something is legal that it is moral. Too many litigators seem to think if they are paid enough money, or if they need to defend their clients, they can lie to protect the bullies and the harassers of the world without any consequences. A common tactic to use in harassment cases is to "deflect and deny," which often involves a good healthy dose of victim shaming. I see it all the time, even to the point where witnesses commit perjury to avoid the legal consequences of their actions, and many times these lies are suborned by their lawyers. Right and wrong no longer matter. Winning is all that counts.

Attacking the victim has become so bad that one researcher in the EEOC's 2016 *Select Task Force on the Study of Harassment in the Workplace* reported that it would be better for victims of harassment to just keep their mouths shut. Yes, this EEOC researcher actually concluded that it would be better for these victims if they just didn't report the illegal and immoral abuse they suffered due to the retaliation and victim shaming they will most likely suffer. That, of course, comes from good lawyers doing their jobs.

Such retaliation and victim shaming has another critical effect: It scares most of the victim's witnesses into silence. The passive aggressive nature of humans will victimize the victim all over again.

Of course, in today's digital world, this deflect and deny strategy can cause the client more harm than good. Rather than admitting to what the client did then begging for forgiveness and swearing to never do it again, too many lawyers go right to the deflect and deny attack strategy. Of course, once the truth comes out later, the client's reputation is doomed, as we have all seen happen too many times.

That is why good litigators will often settle these cases, but they will also require the victims to never talk about the horrible acts committed by the harasser. This, of course, allows the harasser to move on and commit the same abusive acts all over again against someone else.

Yes, hiding behind one's lawyers is the norm, and that is how litigators can get rich. But then, they are still going to burn in Hell.

I cannot even begin to describe how many times I have spoken up when something I saw was either illegal or unfair, often on a pro bono basis, only to find myself standing there alone to get slaughtered. Almost every time, I hear someone in a position of power actually tell me that they didn't do anything to help because they knew someone would be upset. Well, when we have the rampant bullying that is going on in our workplaces and world today, I think we have some people who might need upsetting.

When I first started my private practice, my wife got me a framed poster with a quote from Dante Alighieri's *Inferno* that says:

> "The hottest places in Hell are reserved for those who, in times of great moral crisis, maintain their neutrality."

These are the words I live by every day of my life.

Can One Person Make a Difference?

AUTHOR'S NOTE: In this final section, you will see many offensive terms and slurs. My apologies ahead of time, but in order to get a true understanding of what Jackie Robinson experienced, and what many still experience today, the historical truth must be told. I am basically following Jabari Asim's lead from his book, *The N Word: Who Can Say It, Who Shouldn't, and Why.* Asim claims that the n-word should only be used in order to give an accurate portrayal of its use as part of our history. Granted, it is a very twisted part of our history, but it is still part of our history, nonetheless.

So, let's say you did speak up when you see bullying. Would it make any difference? Can one person really make a difference?

Absolutely.

For example, in the early 1900's, Branch Rickey was a student at Ohio Wesleyan University. He was given the job of managing the Ohio Wesleyan baseball team, even though he was only 21 years old at the time.[259]

Charles "Tommy" Thomas, a young Black man, was the team's catcher.[260]

In 1903, the Ohio Wesleyan baseball team went to South Bend, Indiana to play the University of Notre Dame. However, a clerk at the Oliver Hotel refused to let Tommy register and stay with the team. So, Rickey told the team's student manager to go to the local YMCA to try to get a room not just for Tommy, but also for the entire team. If Tommy couldn't stay at the Oliver Hotel, then none of them would stay there. Rickey, who was determined to keep his team together, asked to speak to the hotel manager.[261]

After speaking to the manager, he finally agreed to let Tommy wait in Rickey's room until lodging could be found for him in South Bend's Black neighborhood. When he and Tommy got into the room, Rickey called the front desk and ordered a cot. The hotel manager was furious and accused Rickey of breaking his word. However, Rickey, who was not one to be toyed with, shouted back, "Under no circumstances will I leave or allow Thomas to be put out."[262]

However, once the cot was set up, Tommy broke down sobbing and scratching at his skin as if he wanted to remove the color from his hands. "I never felt so helpless in my life," Rickey later said in an interview.[263]

In his later writings, Rickey described what he saw:

"Tommy stood in the corner, tense and brooding and in silence. I asked him to sit in a chair and relax. Instead, he sat on the edge of the cot, his huge shoulders hunched and his large hands clasped between his knees. I couldn't take my gaze from Tommy. Tears welled ... spilled down his Black face and splashed to the floor. Then his shoulders heaved convulsively and he rubbed one great hand over the other with all the power of his body, muttering, 'Black skin ... Black skin. If I could only make 'em White.' He kept rubbing and rubbing as though he would remove the Blackness by sheer friction."[264]

Now, could you imagine hating yourself so much that you are literally ready to peel your own skin off?

Rickey knew that Tommy was good enough to play professional baseball if it wasn't for the color barrier. Rickey tried to console Tommy by telling him that one day, there would be equal opportunity for all baseball players, regardless of their color. He told Tommy to buck up and he promised him they would "lick this one day."[265]

Rickey said that for the rest of his life, he could always see and hear that young man sitting on the edge of that small cot in South Bend, ashamed of who he was and his existence. Rickey said one day he would have the chance to do something about it.[266]

In 1945, Albert Benjamin "Happy" Chandler became the second Commissioner of Major League Baseball, replacing Judge Kenesaw Mountain Landis. Happy Chandler let it be known right away that he was going to be a very different Commissioner of Baseball than Landis, who actively kept Blacks from playing in the White leagues. Chandler said if Negroes could fight and die in Okinawa, Guadalcanal, and in the South Pacific during WWII, they could play baseball in America.[267]

Branch Rickey, who was then part owner, General Manager, and President of the Brooklyn Dodgers, saw his chance. After looking through the files of many Black players, he chose Jackie Robinson.[268]

In 1945, Rickey told Red Barber, who was from Mississippi and the radio voice of the Brooklyn Dodgers, that he was going to break baseball's color line.[269]

The news stunned Barber. Barber later said, "This is something I had never even dreamed of and it was a shock to me." Barber went home that evening and considered resigning as the voice of the Dodgers, rather than working for an integrated team.[270]

Rickey then asked Jackie Robinson to come and see him in Brooklyn.[271]

Rickey knew Jackie could play, but what he really needed to know is if he could take the abuse he would get. Rickey had carefully selected Jackie for this part. The main question Rickey had was whether Jackie could weather the storm of taunts and abuse that were going to be hurled at him being a Black player in major league baseball.[272]

On August 28, 1945, Jackie came to the Brooklyn Dodgers' office to meet with Rickey.[273] Jackie had no idea what Rickey had in mind. Rickey told him that he was looking for the right Black ball player to sign a contract not with the Negro League team in Brooklyn, but instead with the White Brooklyn Dodgers.[274]

The entire meeting centered on whether Jackie could control himself for the terrible abuse he would endure. Rickey then did everything he could to provoke him.

Jackie was known for having a temper and Rickey was concerned. Even his Black teammates on the Kansas City Monarchs were not sure if he could control himself when he was attacked in the majors. Jackie knew how to fight and he would fight.[275]

Rickey was a man who never used profanity. In fact, the strongest expression he ever used was "Judas Priest." However, on that day, he called Jackie every foul thing he could think of to test him. He repeatedly asked Jackie, "Can you take it? Can you not retaliate when a player spikes you, when opponents or even teammates call you names? When restaurants on our road trips won't serve you? Are you my champion?" [276]

"Suppose I collide with you at second base. When I get up, I yell, 'You dirty, Black son of a bitch!" as he yelled right into Jackie's face.[277]

Rickey then calmed a bit and asked Jackie, "What do you do?"[278]

Jackie was stunned. All he could do was blink, lick his lips, and swallow.[279]

After a few seconds, Jackie finally answered, "Mr. Rickey, do you want a ballplayer who's afraid to fight back?"[280]

Rickey roared back, "I want a ballplayer with guts enough *not* to fight back."[281]

Rickey told Jackie that it was critical he found a player who would not strike back. He told Jackie that they can't win this with retaliation. Rickey then paced about the room, turned and pointed his finger at Jackie and said, "You've got to do this job with base hits and stolen bases and fielding ground balls, Jackie. Nothing else!"[282]

By now, Rickey's face was covered in sweat and he was just inches from Jackie's. Rickey then shouted, "So, what if I haul off and punch you right in the cheek!" At that instant, Rickey swung his huge fist at Jackie, barely missing his face. Jackie blinked, but he did not move.[283]

"What do you do?" Rickey asked.[284]

"Mr. Rickey," he said. "I've got two cheeks. That it?"[285]

Jackie assured Rickey that he was the champion he needed. Rickey believed him, but he made Jackie promise that he would not fight back for his first three seasons, no matter what unimaginable things happened to him. Jackie agreed.[286]

So, on October 23, 1945, the Dodgers announced that Jackie would be playing for the Montreal Royals of the Class AAA International League, a farm affiliate of the Brooklyn Dodgers for the 1946 season.[287]

However, not everyone with the Royals was thrilled about Jackie coming to play there, namely Clay Hopper, the team's manager. When Hopper, who was from Mississippi, said that he did not want to be the manager of an integrated team, Rickey did not back down. Jackie was coming to Montreal. To that, Hopper replied, "Do you really think a nigger is a human being?"[288]

In 1946, Jackie began playing for the Montreal Royals. Right away, the abuse started, and it was relentless. Whenever the Royals were on the road, fans and other teams would yell slurs and insults at him. As the season went on and the abuse continued, he was racked with stomach pains. At one point, he almost suffered a nervous breakdown.[289]

The Royals won the Minor League World Series that year. When Jackie left the stadium after the final game of the series, he was chased three blocks by adoring White fans wanting to congratulate him rather than hurt him.[290]

Jackie led the International League that year with a batting average of .349 and a fielding percentage of .985. He was also named the league's Most Valuable Player.[291]

After the season was over, Clay Hopper, the manager who questioned Jackie's humanity, urged Rickey to bring him up to the Dodgers for the 1947 season.[292]

Not surprisingly, some of the Dodgers were not too happy about playing on the same team as a Black man in 1947. Bobby Bragan, a backup catcher, Eddie Stanky, the starting second baseman, and Dixie Walker, the Dodgers star outfielder, to mention a few, started a petition to keep Jackie from joining the team. The petition said: "If you promote a Black man [Robinson], we will not play."[293]

The team's captain, Harold "Pee Wee" Reese, a southerner from Kentucky, had grown up under the rules of segregation and Jim Crow. But he'd also served in the Navy during World War II, so he saw first-hand the negative consequences racism could have on people. Reese refused to sign the petition, explaining later that he simply thought Robinson "had a right to be there."[294]

When Reese was reminded that Jackie was a shortstop and that was his position, he replied, "If he is good enough to take my job, then he is entitled to it."[295]

When Rickey heard about the petition, he turned to his manager, Leo Durocher, and told him, "Stomp this fire out right now because we can't let it spread."[296]

Leo "The Lip" Durocher was known for speaking his mind. Durocher got the Dodger players out of bed in the middle of the night to hold his meeting. Durocher, of course, cussed them out and then told them, "I'll tell you what you can do with your petition. If a guy can win games for me, I don't care if he's White, or Black, or striped, or green, he's going to play for me. I'm the manager of this team, and I say he plays. What's more, I say he can make us all rich. And if any of you cannot use the money, I will see that you are all traded."[297]

He also told the players that Jackie was coming, and they'd better get used to it because there were going to be a lot more Black players coming right behind him.[298]

When the Philadelphia Phillies came to town to play the Dodgers in a three-game series in April 1947, Ben Chapman, the Phillies' manager, led his team in a hailstorm of racial abuse directed right at Jackie. Up to that point, it was the worst abuse he had ever experienced.[299]

For the next two days, Chapman and the Phillies rained their abuse down on Jackie. When Jackie came up to bat, the Phillies started it all over again, calling him "Nigger trash!"[300]

Jackie took it all in silence.[301]

Finally, one Dodger couldn't take it anymore and shouted into the Phillies dugout: "Listen, you yellow-bellied cowards, why don't you yell at someone who can answer back?"[302]

Robinson's defender was Eddie Stanky, one of the founders of the petition.

Later in the game, when Dixie Walker made it to first base, he also chastised Chapman for the way he was abusing Jackie.[303]

This experience in Philadelphia was a turning point for Jackie and the Dodgers. Chapman had inadvertently rallied the Dodgers around Jackie. The Dodgers players, seeing how Jackie held his temper and took the abuse, now admired him. Since he could not lash back, his White teammates were ready to do it for him.[304]

Years later, Rickey said, "Chapman did more than anybody to unite the Dodgers. When he poured out that string of unconscionable abuse, he solidified and unified thirty men, not one of whom was willing to sit by and see someone kick around a man who had his hands tied behind his back. Chapman made Jackie a real member of the Dodgers."[305]

After the series ended, Chapman was hounded mercilessly by the media and by fans who were appalled by his racist behavior. Chapman was ordered to pose in a photograph with Robinson as a conciliatory gesture when the two teams met in Philadelphia in May of 1947. The photo op was staged to show the world that the incident was addressed and supposedly resolved. It was an attempt to repair the Phillies' damaged image and Chapman's job was on the line. Being the emotionally intelligent man he was, Jackie agreed to take the photo and kept Chapman from getting fired. However, since Chapman refused to shake Robinson's hand for the photo, they held onto the same bat so they did not have to touch each other.[306]

Dixie Walker, on the other hand, saw the humor in all of this and said, "I never thought I'd see old Ben eat shit like that."[307]

On May 14, 1947, the Dodgers traveled to Crosley Field in Cincinnati, Ohio to play the Reds. Again, the taunting was almost unbelievable. As Jackie took his position at first base for infield practice, the shouting began. This harassment did not consist of a few isolated heckles from a few loudmouths. Instead, the entire stadium was filled with people yelling obscenities at Jackie. It was also not just the men raining down these insults, but so were the women and children, regardless of age. Fans started calling Jackie all kinds of horrible racial slurs. Some of the Cincinnati players also started shouting racial slurs at Jackie.[308]

At that point, Pee Wee Reese, the Dodgers' all-star shortstop, team captain and a very popular Kentuckian, stopped the Dodgers' warm up. Reese then casually walked over to Jackie where he simply put his arm around Jackie's shoulders.[309]

Reese was one of the most popular players of his day and everyone knew him as the "Little Colonel." Not only was he the Dodgers' captain, but he also assumed some of the managerial duties, like bringing the Dodgers' lineup card to the umpires before the game started.[310]

According to sportswriter Roger Kahn, Reese "looked into the Cincinnati dugout and the grandstands beyond" as the slurs continued to spew throughout Crosley Field. Reese took a relaxed approach. He did not call anyone out. He just kept his arm firmly around Jackie's shoulders. This small gesture of support from the all-star Kentuckian soon quieted the crowd and defused the rush of hate directed towards Jackie.[311]

Amazingly, this show of support from Kentucky's most famous and revered baseball player of his time caused a hush to fall over Crosley Field. Reese's message was clear: This is my friend.[312]

For both Jackie and Reese, this moment bonded them for life. It also had a lasting impact on Jackie's ability to better deal with the horrendous physical and mental abuse that was to come. Years later, Jackie told Roger Kahn: "After Reese came over like that, I never felt alone on a baseball field again."[313]

In August 1947, the Dodgers were visiting the reigning World Series Champion, the St. Louis Cardinals. Future Hall of Famer, Enos "Country" Slaughter, hit an infield grounder and was thrown out by at least ten feet when he jumped into the air and spiked Jackie's thigh, slicing open a seven-inch gash. Jackie's White teammates rushed out to see him. The Dodgers were so incensed that they wanted to immediately retaliate against Slaughter, but Jackie called them off. Again, Jackie's control once again showed everyone there was a better way to combat bigotry.[314]

In the end, Jackie and all of the brave individuals who chose not to remain silent, the bystanders who spoke up and chose not to be enablers, changed the world.

Today, major league baseball is one of the most integrated sports on the planet. If you are good enough to make it, you can play. Baseball today has players, coaches, and managers who are White, Black, Hispanic, Asian, and some players who are a little bit of everything. Several countries are now represented in the major leagues, which includes the Dominican Republic, Venezuela, Cuba, Japan, South Korea, and Taiwan. All of this has happened because of what Jackie Robinson did with some simple gestures of support from everyday people. [315]

Heroes!

This story has everything in it. It is full of regular people proudly doing some of the most evil things you can think of to each other. It also has a full cast of enablers, people who just went along with the crowd because it was easy.

But it is also filled with great examples of bystanders who did intervene when it was needed, some in large ways and some in small ones.

And perhaps most importantly, it shows that Henry David Thoreau's civil disobedience, or what John Lewis called "good trouble," has the power to not only change the world one person at a time, but it can turn villains into heroes.

Just as with Frank Meeink, there are unlikely heroes in this story, too. No one ordered these men to be more accepting of Jackie. They became accepting of him by getting to know him, which neurologically rewired them. That is how acceptance ALWAYS works: You get to know the other person and your biases start to drift away.

You should notice that the vast majority of the people who opposed the integration of White major league baseball in 1947 were born and raised in the South. That is usually neither a good nor bad thing, but during the 1910s, 1920s, and 1930s, which is when most of these people were growing up, the South was much more radical than it is now, about 100 years later. This gives us a very strong indication of maybe what these ball players had been told from even before they were born. Many of them were primed with horrible racist beliefs, so what they were doing and saying was common sense to them. Since they had never spent much time around anyone of color, they believed all of the racist myths they had been told.

Try to imagine what it was like for them to realize that everything their parents had ever told them was wrong. Think of what must have gone through their minds when they saw that Jackie Robinson did not fit with all the bigoted tales they had always been told. These were major revelations for them to experience, just like it was for Frank Meeink and Tony.

Red Barber, who considered resigning when he found out that Rickey was going to integrate the Dodgers, said, "Robinson did more for me than I did for him. I had to change my outlook on racial equations, because being raised in the South, when the Black ballplayer came, I had to begin thinking differently. I had to understand with clear eyes that I should and must accept him equally as I did other players. So, to me, it matured me."[316]

Jackie's effect on the founders of the petition, Bobby Bragan, Eddie Stanky, and Dixie Walker, was tremendous.

Jackie Robinson changed Bobby Bragan's life forever. Bragan later said, "After just one road trip, I saw the quality of Jackie the man and the player. I then told Mr. Rickey I had changed my mind and I was honored to be a teammate of Jackie Robinson."[317]

When Bragan attended Rickey's funeral in 1965, he said he wanted to attend because, "Branch Rickey made me a better man."[318]

Later, Bragan became a manager and earned the reputation for being a color-blind leader. When he was the manager of the Dodgers' AAA Spokane Indians farm club in 1959, he played a key role in developing the future all-star Maury Wills, who was Black, into not only an All-Star shortstop but a legend of the stolen base. At the time, Wills' baseball career had stalled in the Dodgers' farm system until he learned how to switch hit under Bragan. The Dodgers' General Manager, Buzzie Bavasi said, "Bobby would call six times a day and tell me over again how Wills had learned to switch-hit and how he was a great team leader, off and on the field, and how I was absolutely nuts if I didn't bring him up right away." When Wills batted .313 in 48 games with Spokane in 1959, he was brought up to the Dodgers in June and won the starting shortstop job.

Wills played in the majors for another 14 years, was on three world championship teams, was elected to the National League All-Star team seven times, and won the National League's Most Valuable Player Award in 1962. Wills also led the league six times in stolen bases and set a new major league record for stolen bases in a single season with 104, ironically breaking Ty Cobb's record of 96 stolen bases set in 1915, who was arguably the most racist man to ever play professional baseball.

Of course, Eddie Stanky's reputation was forever saved because of the times he stood up for Jackie when he couldn't do it for himself.

Not only was Dixie Walker one of the players who stood up for Jackie when he was being attacked by other teams and their fans, but he also helped Jackie with his hitting. Jackie acknowledged how grateful he was for the batting tips Walker gave to him when he was struggling at the plate.[319]

At the end of the 1947 season, Walker said, "No other ball player on this club has done more to put the Dodgers up in the race as Robinson has. He is everything Branch Rickey said he was."[320]

Later, Walker said that starting that petition was "the stupidest thing I've ever done." Walker then asked sportswriter

Roger Kahn that, if he had the opportunity, if he would also write that he was sorry and wanted to apologize for what he had done.[321]

Even Ben Chapman, the poster child for baseball's racist attitudes at the time, changed the way he viewed himself, Blacks, and the world. In the 1990's, Chapman told journalist Ray Robinson, "A man learns about things and mellows as he grows older. I think maybe I've mellowed. Maybe I went too far in those days, when I thought it was OK to try to throw guys off-balance and upset them with jockeying. I'm sorry for many of the things I said. I guess the world changes and maybe I've changed, too."[322]

Chapman then proudly reflected on the success of his son, who was then coaching Black players on an integrated football team. Chapman said, "Look, I'm real proud I've raised my son different. And he gets along well with them. They like him. That's a nice thing, don't you think?"[323]

CLOSING THOUGHTS

After more than ten years of working on this book, I was finishing up the last little bits to send it off to be published when the world seemed to explode in front of my eyes.

- Extremists attacked our Capitol Building while Congress was in session, which not only cost millions of dollars to clean up and repair, but several people were seriously injured and others died.
- A 22-year-old female, Miya Ponsetto, falsely accused a 14-year-old black teenager of stealing her cell phone. She then tackled him as she tried to get the phone from him and later claimed that she could not be a racist because she herself is a "woman of color."
- Another police officer, Adam Coy, shot and killed Andre Hill, an unarmed Black man who was only holding his cell phone in Columbus, Ohio.

And on and on it goes.

After reading this book, I hope you not only have a better understanding as to how and why these tragedies keep occurring, but more importantly, I want you to see what we all need to do individually to keep them from happening in the first place. This is a critical time not just for our workplaces, but for our country and our world.

The Five Skills of Tolerance are not just good rules for building a safe and trusting workplace, but these are critical life skills we all need to use in every aspect of our lives. Please take the time to learn them, practice them, and pass them onto others. When you are done reading this book, give it to someone else. Teach these skills to your children. Implement them in your workplaces. If the good people of the world, the 95 percenters, can practice these Five Skills of Tolerance, then maybe, just maybe, we will not see quite so many bad things happening in our lives. Remember:

> **You will never end bigotry for anyone until you end it for everyone.**

Review Inquiry

Hey, it's Scott here.

I hope you've enjoyed the book, finding it both useful and fun. I have a favor to ask you.

Would you consider giving it a rating wherever you bought the book? Online book stores are more likely to promote a book when they feel good about its content, and reader reviews are a great barometer for a book's quality.

So please go to the website of wherever you bought the book, search for my name and the book title, and leave a review. If able, perhaps consider adding a picture of you holding the book. That increases the likelihood that your review will be accepted!

Many thanks in advance,

Scott Warrick

WILL YOU SHARE THE LOVE?

Get this book for a friend, associate, or family member!

If you have found this book valuable and know others who would find it useful, consider buying them a copy as a gift. Special bulk discounts are available if you would like your whole team or organization to benefit from reading this. Just contact Scott Warrick at scott@scottwarrick.com or visit his website at www.scottwarrick.com.

Would You Like Scott Warrick to Speak to Your Organization?

Book Scott Now!

Scott accepts a limited number of speaking/coaching/training engagements each year. To learn how you can bring his message to your organization, just email Scott at scott@scottwarrick.com. You can always contact Scott and find much more information on this book and many other topics at www.scottwarrick.com.

ENDNOTES

1. Daniel Goleman, *Social Intelligence: The New Science of Human Relationships* (New York, NY, Bantam, 2006), 293.
2. Ruth Umh, "How Diversity Heads Are Steering Their Companies Through The COVID-19 Crisis," *Forbes*, April 16, 2020, accessed September 19, 2020. https://www.forbes.com/sites/ruthumoh/2020/04/15/how-chief-diversity-officers-are-steering-their-companies-through-the-covid-19-crisis/#56cfcbd065a9.
3. Chai Feldblum and Victoria Lipnic, *EEOC Select Task Force on the Study of Harassment in the Workplace: report of co-chairs Chai R. Feldblum & Victoria A. Lipnic,* 2016.
4. Kamala Harris, Twitter Post, February 24, 2017, 11:09 PM. https://twitter.com/KamalaHarris.
5. "Fight for Equality," GLAAD. https://www.glaad.org/resources/ally/10#:~:text=Fight%20for%20Equality%20Lesbian%2C%20gay%2C%20bisexual%20and%20transgender,sexual%20orientation%20and%20gender%20identity%20is%20still%20legal, accessed September 26, 2020.
6. "Hate Map," Southern Poverty Law Center, https://www.splcenter.org/hate-map, accessed September 26, 2020.
7. Amir Vera and Laura Ly, "White woman who called police on a black man bird-watching in Central Park has been fired," CNN, Revised May 26, 2020. https://www.cnn.com/2020/05/26/us/central-park-video-dog-video-african-american-trnd/index.html, accessed September 27, 2020.
8. Ibid.
9. Ibid.
10. Ibid.
11. Ibid.
12. April Siese, "White woman fired from her job after she called the cops on a black man in Central Park," CBS News, May 27, 2020, accessed September 25, 2020. https://www.cbsnews.com/news/central-park-karen-amy-cooper-white-

woman-calls-cops-Black-man-fired-franklin-templeton/, accessed September 25, 2020.
13. Ibid.
14. Ibid; "Amy Cooper (Central Park Karen)," *Vantu News.* https://www.vantunews. com/wiki/biography-amy-cooper-central-park-karen, accessed September 25, 2020.
15. Rebecca Rosenberg, "Manhattan DA charges Amy Cooper over viral Central Park 911 call, *New York Post.* https://nypost.com/2020/07/06/ manhattan-da-charges-amy-cooper-over-viral-central-park-911-call/, accessed September 25, 2020.
16. Ibid.
17. Monica Showalter, "Turns out 'Central Park Karen' was an Obama and Buttigieg donor," *American Thinker.* May 27, 2020. https://www.americanthinker.com/ blog/2020/05/turns_out_central_park_karen_was_an_obama_and_ buttigieg_donor.html, accessed September 25, 2020.
18. Ibid.
19. Travis Bradberry and Jean Greaves, *The Emotional Intelligence Quick Book* (New York: Fireside, 2005), 125, 135-136.
20. Ibid.
21. Ibid.
22. Ibid.
23. Iain Riddick, *Seconds from Disaster, episode 44, Space Shuttle Challenger,* aired January 31, 2007 on National Geographic.
24. Ibid.
25. Ibid.
26. Ibid.
27. Bradberry and Greaves, 125, 135-136.
28. Ibid.
29. Ibid.
30. Ibid.
31. Riddick, *Seconds from Disaster. Space Shuttle Challenger.*
32. Ibid.
33. Sid Bennett, *Seconds from Disaster, Columbia's Last Flight,* aired June 25, 2005 on National Geographic.
34. Ibid.
35. Ibid.
36. Ibid.
37. Ibid.
38. Ibid.
39. Ibid.

40. Ibid.
41. Bradberry and Greaves, 125, 135-136.
42. Bennett, *Seconds from Disaster, Columbia's Last Flight.*
43. Ibid.
44. Ibid.
45. Bradberry and Greaves, 125, 135-136.
46. Sharon Wong, "Making Space for Everyone: The Diversity Journal at NASA Goddard," October 19, 2007, Society for Human Resource Management's National Diversity Conference, Philadelphia, Pennsylvania.
47. Ibid.
48. NASA's "Goddard Space Flight Center Diversity Programs" DDP Handout.
49. Ibid.
50. A base pair (bp) is a unit consisting of two nucleobases bound to each other by hydrogen bonds; "Cracking the Code of Life," PBS, 2001, accessed September 20, 2020. https://www.pbs.org/wgbh/nova/genome/.; "Human Genome Project FAQ," National Human Genome Research Institute, updated February 24, 2020, accessed September 20, 2020. https://www.genome.gov/human-genome-project/Completion-FAQ.
51. "Human Genome Project FAQ."
52. "Economic Impact of the Human Genome Project," Battelle (PDF), accessed August 1, 2013; "Human Genome Project FAQ."
53. Wynne Parry, "Age Confirmed for 'Eve' Mother of All Humans," *Live Science*, August 18, 2010, accessed September 21, 2020. https://www.livescience.com/10015-age-confirmed-eve-mother-humans.html.
54. Susan Bell, "Researcher uses DNA to demonstrate just how closely everyone on Earth is related to everyone else," August 8, 2013, accessed September 20, 2020. https://phys.org/news/2013-08-dna-earth.html.
55. Cecil Adams, "2, 4, 8, 16, ... how can you always have MORE ancestors as you go back in time?" *The Straight Dope*, August 21, 1987, accessed September 20, 2020. https://web.archive.org/web/20041204081025/https://www.straightdope.com/classics/a2_083b.html.
56. Jeremy Thomson, "Humans did come out of Africa, says DNA." *Nature*, December 7, 2000, accessed September 20, 2020. https://www.nature.com/articles/news001207-8; Max Ingman, Henrik Kaessmann, Svante Pääba, Ulf Gyllensten, "Mitochondrial genome variation and the origin of modern humans," Nature, Vol. 408 (2000), 708 - 713.
57. Michael Muehlenbein. "Human Evolutionary Biology," *Cambridge University Press*, 192-213; Stephanie Pappas, "Odd Cause of Humans' Dark Skin Proposed," *Live Science*, February 26, 2014, accessed September 20, 2020. https://www.livescience.com/43674-cancer-skin-color-evolution.html.

58. Daniel Goleman. *Social Intelligence*, 40.

59. Goleman. 40, footnote 5.

60. Goleman, 299.

61. Goleman, 40, footnote 5

62. Kristen Domonell, "This Is Your Body On Fear," *UW Medicine*, October 25, 2017, accessed September 20, 2020, https://rightasrain.uwmedicine.org/well/health/your-body-fear-anxiety#:~:text=Fear%20kicks%20your%20fight%2Dor,including%20the%20amygdala%E2%80%94take%20over; "Fight-or-Flight Reaction," *Changing Minds*, accessed January 26, 2017. http://changingminds.org/explanations/brain/fight_flight.htm.

63. Malcolm Gladwell, *Blink* (Little, Brown, and Co., New York, NY, 2005), 224-228.

64. Domonell, "This Is Your Body On Fear."

65. Ibid.

66. Ibid.

67. Ibid.

68. Joseph LeDoux, *The Emotional Brain* (New York: Simon and Schuster, 1996), 205; Daniel Goleman, *Emotional Intelligence* (New York: Bantam, 1998), 15, 18-20.

69. Anando, "It's now a proven fact – Your unconscious mind is running your life!" *Life Trainings*, accessed on January 22, 2017. http://www.lifetrainings.com/Your-unconscious-mind-is-running-you-life.html

70. Riz Pasha, "57 Dr. Bruce Lipton Quotes on the Biology of Belief," *Succeed Feed*, January 30, 2020, accessed September 20, 2020. https://succeedfeed.com/dr-bruce-lipton-quotes/#:~:text=One%20of%20Dr.%20Bruce%20Lipton%E2%80%99s%20key%20lessons%20is,5%25%20of%20our%20thoughts%20throughout%20any%20given%20day.

71. Goleman, *Social Intelligence*, 40.

72. Jennifer Eberhardt, *Biased: Uncovering the Hidden Prejudice That Shapes What We See, Think, and Do* (New York, NY: Viking, 2019), 31-32.

73. Lisa Marshall, "Speeches: For the average person speaking at a normal pace, what is the average pace, what is the typical number of words they can say in a minute," March 10, 2011, accessed January 21, 2017. https://www.quora.com/Speeches-For-the-average-person-speaking-at-a-normal-pace-what-is-the-typical-number-of-words-they-can-say-in-one-minute.

74. Eberhardt, 31, 35.

75. John Bargh, Mark Chen & Lara Burrows, "Automaticity of social behavior: Direct effects of trait construct and stereotype activation on action," *Journal of Personality and Social Psychology*, 71 (1996): 240.

76. Ibid.

77. Ibid.
78. Ibid.
79. Ibid.
80. Ibid.
81. Ibid.
82. Ibid.
83. The Kirwan Institute for the Study of Race and Ethnicity is a research institute at The Ohio State University. The Kirwan Institute works toward achieving their mission by educating the public, building the capacity of allied social justice organizations, and investing in efforts that support equity and inclusion. Most importantly, the Kirwan Institute's research is designed to be actively used to solve problems in society.
84. Jennifer Eberhardt, Phillip Atiba Goff, Valerie Purdie, & Paul Davies, "Seeing Black: Race, Crime, and Visual Processing," *Journal of Personality and Social Psychology* 87, 6 (2004): 876-893.
85. Ibid.
86. James Brockmole, "Holding A Toy Gun Makes You Think Others Are Too, New Research Shows," *Notre Dame News*, March 19, 2012, accessed September 22, 2020. https://news.nd.edu/news/holding-a-gun-makes-you-think-others-are-too-new-research-shows/.
87. Justine Levinson, "Forgotten Racial Equality: Implicit Bias, Decision making, and Misremembering," *Duke Law Journal* 57, 2 (2007): 345-424.
88. Samuel Sommers, "On Racial Diversity and Group Decision Making: Identifying Multiple Effects of Racial Composition on Jury Deliberations," *Journal of Personality and Social Psychology*, 90, 4 (2006): 597-612.
89. Samuel Sommers & Phoebe Ellsworth, "Race in the Courtroom: Perceptions of Guilt and Dispositional Attributions," *Personality and Social Psychology Bulletin* 26, 11 (2000): 1367-1379. Samuel Sommers & Phoebe Ellsworth, "White Juror Bias: An Investigation of Prejudice Against Black Defendants in the American Courtroom," *Psychology, Public Policy, and Law* 7, 1 (2001): 201-229.
90. Dana Ford. Juror: "'No Doubt' that George Zimmerman Feared for His Life," CNN, July 16, 2013, accessed September 15, 2020. http://www.cnn.com/2013/07/15/justice/zimmerman-juror-book/index.html.
91. Ginger Thompson & Garry Pierre-Pierre, "Portrait of Slain Immigrant: Big Dreams and a Big Heart," *New York Times*, February 12, 1999, accessed August 22, 2017. https://www.nytimes.com/1999/02/12/nyregion/portrait-of-slain-immigrant-big-dreams-and-a-big-heart.html ; "About Amadou," *The Amadou Diallo Foundation*, accessed July 19, 2020. https://www.amadoudiallo.com/about-amadou/.

92. Beth Roy. *41 Shots … and Counting* (Syracuse, NY: Syracuse University Press, 2009), 38.

93. Ginger Thompson & Garry Pierre-Pierre, "Portrait of Slain Immigrant: Big Dreams and a Big Heart," *New York Times*, February 12, 1999, accessed August 22, 2017. https://www.nytimes.com/1999/02/12/nyregion/portrait-of-slain-immigrant-big-dreams-and-a-big-heart.html; Jane Fritsch, "The Diallo Verdict: The Overview; 4 Officers In Diallo Shooting Are Acquitted Of All Charges," *The New York Times*, February 26, 2000, accessed August 22,2017. https://www.nytimes.com/2000/02/26/nyregion/diallo-verdict-overview-4-officers-diallo-shooting-are-acquitted-all-charges.html

94. 94. Roy, 10.

95. Juan Forero, "Serial Rapist Gets 155 Years; Judge Suggests His Crimes Contributed to Diallo Shooting," *The New York Times*, August 2, 2000, accessed July 19, 2020. https://www.nytimes.com/2000/08/02/nyregion/serial-rapist-gets-155-years-judge-suggests-his-crimes-contributed-diallo.html.

96. Fritsch, "The Diallo Verdict."

97. 97. Roy, 10.

98. Fritsch, "The Diallo Verdict."

99. Gladwell, 189.

100. Andrea Reiher, "What Happened to Amadou Diallo's Killers?" *Heavy*, May 11, 2020, accessed July 19, 2020. https://heavy.com/entertainment/2020/05/amadou-diallo-police-officers-killers/.

101. Garrett Bradley, *Trial by Media, 3, 41 Shots*, aired May 11, 2020, on Netflix. https://www.netflix.com/watch/81025116?trackId=200257859.

102. Roy, 44-46.

103. Roy, 38.

104. Fritsch, "The Diallo Verdict."

105. Juan Forero, "Serial Rapist Gets 155 Years; Judge Suggests His Crimes Contributed to Diallo Shooting," *New York Times*, August 2, 2000, accessed July 19, 2020. https://www.nytimes.com/2000/08/02/nyregion/serial-rapist-gets-155-years-judge-suggests-his-crimes-contributed-diallo.html

106. Gladwell, 224-228.

107. Roy, 46.

108. Lauren McGuire, "Who would you shoot?" *The Society Pages*, July 15, 2013, accessed July 19, 2020. https://thesocietypages.org/socimages/2013/07/15/guest-post-who-would-you-shoot/#:~:text=In%202002%2C%20a%20study%20by%20Joshua%20Correll%20and,a%20wallet%29%20in%20a%20video%20game%20style%20setting.; Joshua Correll, Bernadette Park, Charles M. Judd and Bernd Wittenbrink, "The Police Officer's Dilemma: Using Ethnicity to

Disambiguate Potentially Threatening Individuals," *Journal of Personality and Social Psychology* 83, 6, (2002) 1314 -1329.

109. Correll, Park, Judd and Wittenbrink, "The Police Officer's Dilemma."

110. McGuire, "Who would you shoot?"; Correll, Park, Judd and Wittenbrink, "The Police Officer's Dilemma."

111. Correll, Park, Judd and Wittenbrink, "The Police Officer's Dilemma."

112. "CBS News Investigates Police Reforms Including Implicit-Bias Training," CBS News, aired August 7, 2019, accessed August 8, 2019. https://www. cbsnews. com/video/ policing-in-america-evaluating-implicit-bia s-training-five-years-after-michael-browns-death/

113. Ibid.

114. Ibid.

115. Goleman. *Emotional Intelligence*, 165-183; Robert Sapolsky. *Stress and Your Body: Stress, Learning and Memory*. (Chantilly, VA: The Teaching Company, 2010), accessed January 22, 2017; Robert Sapolsky. *Stress and Your Body: Stress and the Biology of Depression*. (Chantilly, VA: The Teaching Company, 2010), accessed January 22, 2017.

116. Pamela Kulbarsh, "2015 Police Suicide Statistics," January 15, 2016, accessed January 1, 2021. https://www.officer.com/training-careers/article/1215662 2/2015-police-suicide-statistics.

117. "5 Common Causes of PTSD in Law Enforcement," Outside the Badge, accessed January 1, 2021. https://outsidethebadge.com/ptsd-police-officer/#:~:text=It%20is%20estimated%20that%20almost%20 20%20percent%20of,PTSD%20 for%20members%20of%20the%20law%20 enforcement%20community

118. Eberhardt, 39.

119. Anthony Greenwald, Debbie McGhee and Jordan Schwartz, "Measuring Individual Differences in Implicit Cognition: The Implicit Association Test," *Journal of Personality and Social Psychology* 74, 6 (1998), 1464-1480; Eberhardt, 39.

120. Ibid.

121. Ibid.

122. Daniel Goleman, *Social Intelligence*, 9.

123. Jeanette Nordon, *Understanding The Human Brain: Lecture 26: Brain Plasticity* (Chantilly, VA: The Teaching Company, 2007).

124. LeDoux, 157, footnote 15.

125. LeDoux, 299.

126. Goleman, 303; Thomas Pettigrew, "The ultimate attribution error: Extending Allport's cognitive analysis of prejudice." *Personality and Social Psychology Bulletin* 5, 4 (1979): 461-476.

127. Ibid.

128. Ibid.
129. Goleman, 301.
130. Ibid.
131. Gladwell, 96-98
132. Pasha, "57 Dr. Bruce Lipton Quotes."
133. Victoria Taylor, "Unhappy in America: Nearly 70% of U.S. employees miserable at work, study finds," *New York Daily News*, January 28, 2015, accessed September 5, 2020. https://www.nydailynews.com/life-style/majority-u-s-workers-not-engaged-job-gallup-poll-article-1.2094990.
134. Clarisse Levitan. "Why 85% of People Hate their Jobs," *Staff Squared*, December 3, 2019, accessed September 4, 2019. https://www.staffsquared. com/blog/why-85-of-people-hate-their-jobs/.
135. Jim Clifton, "The World's Broken Workplace," Gallup, published June 13, 2017, accessed September 5, 2020. https://news. gallup.com/opinion/chairman/212045/world-broken-workplace. aspx?g_source=position1&g_medium=related&g_campaign=tiles.
136. United States Department of Labor, Workplace Violence, Occupational Safety and Health Administration, accessed January 28, 2017.
137. Douglas Fields, "Humans Are Genetically Predisposed to Kill Each Other," *Psychology Today*, October 2, 2016, accessed October 15, 2017. https://www.psychologytoday.com/us/blog/the-new-brain/201610/humans-are-genetically-predisposed-kill-each-other.
138. Aamer Madhani, "University of Missouri fires professor Melissa Click," *USA TODAY*, February 25, 2016, accessed September 3, 2020. https://www.usatoday.com/story/news/2016/02/25/university-missouri-fires-professor-melissa-click/80940690/.
139. Geeta Gandbhir & Sam Pollard, *Why We Hate, 3, Tools and Tactics*, aired October 27, 2019, accessed from https://www.netflix.com.
140. Ibid.
141. Ibid.
142. Gregory Gordon. "Atrocity Speech Law: Foundation, Fragmentation, Fruition," *Oxford University Press*, 2017, 286; Gandbhir and Pollard, *Why We Hate, 3, Tools and Tactics*.
143. Gandbhir and Pollard, *Why We Hate, 3, Tools and Tactics*.
144. Philip Gourevitch, *We Wish to Inform You That Tomorrow We Will Be Killed with Our Families* (Reprinted) (London; New York, N.Y.: Picador, 2000)
145. Gandbhir and Pollard, *Why We Hate, 3, Tools and Tactics*.
146. Ibid.
147. Robert Thsarkissian, "Martin Buber," accessed September 3, 2020. http://www.roberthsarkissian.com/iof/BUBER.HTM

148. Goleman, *Social Intelligence*, 299, footnote 4. Elie Wiesel made these remarks at the sixtieth anniversary of the liberation of Auschwitz. See *Jerusalem Post*, January 25, 2005.
149. Gandbhir and Pollard, *Why We Hate, 3, Tools and Tactics.*
150. Ibid.
151. Ibid.
152. Ibid.
153. Ibid.
154. Ibid.
155. Ibid.
156. Ibid.
157. Ibid.
158. Ibid.
159. Mark Berman, "Prosecutors say Dylann Roof 'self-radicalized' online, wrote another manifesto in jail," *The Washington Post*, August 22, 2016, accessed September 15, 2019. https://www.washingtonpost.com/news/post-nation/wp/2016/08/22/prosecutors-say-accused-charleston-church-gunma n-self-radicalized-online/; Meg Kinnard, "Feds: Church shooting suspect entrenched in his beliefs," *Telegram*, August 23, 2016, accessed September 15, 2019. https://www.telegram.com/news/20160823/feds-church-shooting-suspect-entrenched-in-his-beliefs. Associated Press.
160. Gandbhir and Pollard, *Why We Hate, 3, Tools and Tactics.*
161. Ibid.
162. Ibid.
163. Daniel Goleman, *Working with Emotional Intelligence* (New York: Bantam, 1998), 60; Goleman, *Social Intelligence*, 40.
164. Gandbhir and Pollard, *Why We Hate, 3, Tools and Tactics.*
165. Ibid.
166. Ibid.
167. Ibid.
168. Ibid.
169. Ibid.
170. Ibid.
171. Ibid.
172. Ibid.
173. Ibid.
174. Ibid.
175. Ibid.
176. Ibid.
177. Ibid.

178. Ibid.
179. Ibid.
180. Ibid.
181. Ibid.
182. Ibid.
183. Ibid.
184. Ibid.
185. Ibid.
186. Ibid.
187. Ibid.
188. Ibid.
189. Ibid.
190. Ibid.
191. Goleman, *Social Intelligence*, 306.
192. Gandbhir and Pollard, *Why We Hate, 3, Tools and Tactics.*
193. Eberhardt, 31-32.
194. Ibid.
195. Eberhardt, 24.
196. Eberhardt, 13.
197. Eberhardt, 14.
198. Ibid.
199. Ibid.
200. Eberhardt, 15
201. Eberhardt, 17.
202. Eberhardt, 19.
203. Ibid.
204. Eberhardt, 20.
205. Ibid.
206. Ibid.
207. John Wilson, Kurt Hugnberg, & Nicholas Rule, "Racial Bias in Judgments of Physical Size and Formidability: From Size to Threat," *Journal of Personality and Social Psychology* 113, 1, 59-80, March 13, 2017; "Study Finds Americans See Black Men as Larger And More Threatening Than White Men of The Same Size," *APA*, March 13, 2017, accessed August 20, 2020. https://www.apa. org/ news/press/releases/2017/03/Black-men-threatening.
208. Ibid.
209. Ibid.
210. Ibid.
211. Ibid.
212. Ibid.

213. Ibid.

214. Linda Villarosa, "Myths about physical racial differences were used to justify slavery — and are still believed by doctors today," *New York Times*, August 14, 2019, accessed August 20, 2020. https://www.nytimes.com/interactive/2019/08/14/magazine/racial-differences-doctors.html.

215. Howard Kelly & Walter Burrage, "Sims, James Marion," *American Medical Biographies* (Baltimore: The Norman, Remington Company, 1920); Sarah Spettel & Mark Donald, "The Portrayal of J. Marion Sims' Controversial Surgical Legacy," *The Journal of Urology* 185, 6, 2424-2427, June 2011; Barron Lerner, "Scholars Argue Over Legacy of Surgeon Who Was Lionized, Then Vilified," *The New York Times*, October 28, 2003, accessed August 20, 2020. https://www.nytimes.com/2003/10/28/health/scholars-argue-over-legacy-of-surgeon-who-was-lionized-then-vilified.html.

216. Kelly Hoffman, Sophie Trawalter, Jordan Axt & Norman Oliver, "Racial bias in pain assessment and treatment recommendations, and false beliefs about biological differences between Blacks and Whites," April 4, 2016, accessed August 20, 2020. https://www.pnas.org/content/113/16/4296; Villarosa, "Myths about physical racial differences."

217. Ronald Wyatt, "Pain and Ethnicity," *AMA Journal of Ethics*, May 2013, accessed August 20, 2020. https://journalofethics.ama-assn.org/article/pain-and-ethnicity/2013-05. Villarosa, "Myths about physical racial differences."

218. NBC4 Staff, "Columbus police identify 'person of interest' from protest, attorney calls post 'inaccurate and reckless," NBC News, aired May 31, 2020, accessed June 1, 2020. https://www.nbc4i.com/news/local-news/columbus-police-searching-for-person-of-interest-in-saturdays-protest/.

219. Grant Stringer & Quincy Snowdon, "Unlikely Suspect: Those who knew Elijah balk at Aurora police account of his death," *Sentinel Colorado*, October 27, 2019, accessed July 2, 2020. https://whatiamunity.com/elijah-mcclain/.

220. Ibid.

221. Ibid.

222. Andrew W. Kiragu, "The Death of Elijah McClain-reflections on living with autism while Black," *Minnesota Spokesman Recorder*, July 15, 2020, accessed August 1, 2020. https://spokesman-recorder.com/2020/07/15/the-death-of-elijah-mcclain-reflections-on-living-with-autism-while-Black/; Alexander Narzaryan, "'I'm just different': The family of Elijah McClain, a 23-year-old Black man killed by Colorado cops almost a year ago, is still waiting for justice," *Yahoo News*, June 27, 2020, accessed June 27, 2020. https://news.yahoo.com/im-just-different-the-family-of-elijah-mc-clain-a-23-yearold-Black-man-killed-by-colorado-cops-090048258.html.

223. "Calls for Justice After Elijah McClain's Death Resurfaces," *American Autism Association*, published June 30, 2020, accessed June 30, 2020. https://www.myautism.org/news-features/calls-for-justice-after-elijah-mcclain s-death-resurfaces; Kiragu, "The Death of Elijah McClain."

224. Ibid.

225. Kiragu, "The Death of Elijah McClain."

226. "Calls for Justice After Elijah McClain's Death Resurfaces"; Narzaryan, "I'm just different."

227. Kiragu, "The Death of Elijah McClain." Fitzsimmons, "I'm just different. That's all."

228. Scott Wilson, "Elijah McClain's death reflects failures of White, suburban police departments," *Washington Post*, September 3, 2020, accessed September 3, 2020. https://www.msn.com/en-us/news/us/elijah-mcclains-death-reflects-failures-of-White-suburban-police-departments/ar-BB18EoOJ?li=BBnb7Kz.

229. Kiragu, "The Death of Elijah McClain." Fitzsimmons, "I'm just different. That's all."

230. Ibid.

231. Wilson, "Elijah McClain's death reflects failures of White, suburban police departments."

232. Fitzsimmons, "I'm just different. That's all."

233. Ibid.

234. Narzaryan, "I'm just different."

235. Lucy Tompkins, "Here's What You Need To Know About Elijah McClain's Death," *The New York Times*, August 16, 2020, accessed July 2, 2020. https://www.nytimes.com/article/who-was-elijah-mcclain.html.

236. Ibid.

237. Erik Ortiz, "Elijah McClain was injected with ketamine while hand-cuffed. Some medical experts worry about its use during police calls," NBC News, July 1, 2020, accessed July 31, 2020. https://www.nbc-news.com/news/us-news/elijah-mcclain-was-injected-ketamine-whil e-handcuffed-some-medical-experts-n1232697

238. Kiragu, "The Death of Elijah McClain."

239. Claire Lampe, "What We Know About the Killing of Elijah McClain," *The Cut*, updated August 11, 2020, accessed August 13, 2020; https://www.thecut.com/2020/08/the-killing-of-elijah-mcclain-everything-we-know.html.

240. Feldblum and Lipnic, 56-57.

241. Dorothy Espalage, Therese Pigott, & Joshua Polanin, "A Meta-Analysis of School-Based Bullying Prevention Programs' Effects on Bystander Intervention Behavior," *School Psychology Review* 41, 1 (2012), 47-65.

242. Feldblum and Lipnic, 56-57.
243. Saul McLeod, "The Milgram Shock Experiment," *Simply Psychology*, February 5, 2017, September 19, 2020. https://www.simplypsychology.org/milgram.html.
244. Ibid.
245. Ibid.
246. Ibid.
247. Ibid.
248. Adeel Hassan, "Ohio Doctor Charged With Killing 25 Patients in Fentanyl Overdoses," *The New York Times*, June 5, 2019, accessed September 15, 2020. https://www.nytimes.com/2019/06/05/us/ohio-doctor-murder-fentanyl-overdose.html; John Futty, "Attorney for Dr. Husel plans to build an uncomplicated defense," *The Columbus Dispatch*, January 31, 2020, accessed September 15, 2020. .https://www.dispatch.com/news/20200131/attorney-for-dr-husel-plans-to-build-uncomplicated-defense.
249. Hassan, "Ohio Doctor Charged With Killing 25 Patients."
250. Ibid.
251. Erik Ortiz, "Ohio doctor charged with 25 counts of murder, accused of prescribing excessive doses of painkillers," *NBC News*, June 5, 2019, accessed September 16, 2020. https://www.nbcnews.com/news/us-news/ohio-doctor-charged-25-counts-murder-accused-prescribing-excessive-doses-n970026.
252. Hassan, "Ohio Doctor Charged With Killing 25 Patients."
253. Ellyn Santiago, "William S. Husel: 5 Fast Facts You Need to Know," *Heavy*, June 5, 2019, accessed September 20, 2020. https://heavy.com/news/2019/01/william-s-husel/.
254. Hassan, "Ohio Doctor Charged With Killing 25 Patients."
255. Ibid.
256. Theodore Decker, Joanne Viviano, Mike Wagner, Holly Zachariah, "Former Mount Carmel doctor William Husel has complicated past," *The Columbus Dispatch*, January 31, 2019, accessed September 20, 2020. https://www.dispatch.com/news/20190131/former-mount-carmel-doctor-william-husel-has-complicated-past.
257. Ibid.
258. "USA Gymnastics sex abuse scandal," https://en.wikipedia.org/wiki/USA_Gymnastics_sex_abuse_scandal, accessed January 21, 2020; "Penn State settlements covered 1971 Sandusky abuse claim," *The Associated Press*, May 8, 2016, accessed January 22, 2017. http://www.usatoday.com/story/sports/ncaaf/2016/05/08/penn-state-settlements-jerry-sandusky-joe-paterno/84125254/.

259. Frank Thompson, "Dr. Charles L. Thomas and Branch Rickey: Making Promises and Battling Racism," *All Things Wildly Considered*, July 2, 2017, accessed September 16, 2020. https://allthingswildlyconsidered.blogspot.com/2017/07/dr-charles-l-thomas-and-branch-rickey.html.

260. Ibid.

261. Ibid.

262. Ibid.

263. Ibid.

264. Ibid.

265. Ibid.

266. Ibid.

267. "Jackie Robinson Breaks Baseball's Color Barrier, 1945," *Eye Witness to History*, 2005, accessed September 17, 2020. http://eyewitnesstohistory.com/ robinson.htm; https://en.wikipedia.org/wiki/Happy_Chandler, accessed September 17, 2020; Ken Burns, *Baseball, Episode 6, The National Pastime*. Florentine Films, Baseball Film Project, Inc., and WETA-TV, Aired September 25, 1994 on PBS.

268. "Jackie Robinson," https://en.wikipedia.org/wiki/Jackie_Robinson, accessed September 16, 2020.

269. Burns, *Baseball*.

270. Ibid.

271. "Clyde Sukeforth," https://en.wikipedia.org/wiki/Clyde_Sukeforth, accessed September 18, 2020.

272. "Jackie Robinson."

273. Burns, *Baseball*; "Jackie Robinson."

274. "Jackie Robinson Breaks Baseball's Color Barrier, 1945."

275. Burns, *Baseball*.

276. "Jackie Robinson Breaks Baseball's Color Barrier, 1945."; Burns, *Baseball*; "Jackie Robinson."

277. "Jackie Robinson Breaks Baseball's Color Barrier, 1945."

278. Ibid.

279. Ibid.

280. Ibid.

281. Ibid.

282. Ibid.

283. Ibid.

284. Ibid.

285. Ibid.

286. Ibid.

287. Ibid.; "Jackie Robinson"

288. Burns, *Baseball.*

289. Ibid.

290. Ibid.

291. "Jackie Robinson"

292. Burns, *Baseball.*

293. "Dixie Walker," https://en.wikipedia.org/wiki/Dixie_Walker, accessed September 18, 2020.

294. Carl Cannon, "Jackie Robinson and Remaking of Baseball," *Real Clear History,* April 15, 2013, accessed September 17, 2020. https://www.realclearhistory. com/historiat/2013/04/15/jackie_robinson_and_remaking_of_baseball_105.html.

295. Burns, *Baseball.*

296. "Dixie Walker"; "Jackie Robinson Breaks Baseball's Color Barrier, 1945"; Cannon, "Jackie Robinson and Remaking of Baseball."

297. "Jackie Robinson Breaks Baseball's Color Barrier, 1945."

298. Burns, *Baseball.*

299. Johnny Goodtimes, "Jackie Robinson and the Phillies," *Philly Sports History,* April 15, 2011, accessed September 18, 2020. http://phillysportshistory. com/2011/04/15/jackie-robinson-and-the-phillies/.

300. William Kashatus, "W-B native took a stand against poor treatment of Jackie Robinson," *Citizen's Voice,* April 12, 2014, updated April 17, 2020, accessed September 17, 2020. https://www.citizensvoice.com/lifestyles /w-b-native-took-a-stand-against-poor-treatment-of-jackie-robinson/ article_36cebfd5-2424-5195-8418-0061d9987476.html.

301. Ibid.

302. Andrew Harner, "Jackie Robinson's Struggle as the First Black Player in MLB," April 1, 2020, accessed September 18, 2020. https:// howtheyplay.com/team-sports/Jackie-Robinson-and-the-struggle-o f-becoming-the-first-Black-player-in-Major-League-Baseball.

303. Kashatus, "W-B native took a stand against poor treatment of Jackie Robinson."

304. Ibid.

305. Goodtimes, "Jackie Robinson and the Phillies."

306. Ibid.

307. "Ben Chapman," https://en.wikipedia.org/wiki/Ben_Chapman_(baseball), accessed September 18, 2020.

308. "Jackie Robinson"

309. Jack Doyle, "Reese & Robbie, 1945-2005," *Pop History Dig,* June 29, 2011, updated February 1, 2019, accessed September 16, 2020. https://www.pophistorydig. com/topics/tag/robinson-death-threats/.

310. "Pee Wee Reese," https://en.wikipedia.org/wiki/Pee_Wee_Reese, accessed September 17, 2020.

311. Doyle, "Reese & Robbie, 1945-2005."

312. Burns, *Baseball*.

313. Doyle, "Reese & Robbie, 1945-2005."

314. Burns, *Baseball*.

315. Jens Manual Krogstad, "67 years after Jackie Robinson broke the color barrier, Major League Baseball looks very different," April 16, 2014, accessed September 18, 2020. https://www.pewresearch.org/fact-tank/2014/04/1 6/67-years-after-jackie-robinson-broke-the-color-barrier-major-league-ba seball-looks-very-different/.

316. Burns, *Baseball*.

317. "Bobby Bragan," https://en.wikipedia.org/wiki/Bobby_Bragan#:~:text= Bragan%20had%20clashed%20with%20Rickey%20in%201947%20 over,%2C%20who%20signed%20a%20petition%20against%20 Robinson %27s%20presence, accessed September 17, 2020.

318. Ibid.

319. Lyle Spatz, "Dixie Walker," *Society for American Baseball Research*, accessed September 19, 2020. https://sabr.org/bioproj/person/dixie-walker-2/ #:~:text=The%20relationship%20between%20Dixie%20Walker%20and%20 Jackie%20 Robinson,or%20any%20other%20Black%20man%2C%20as%20 a%20teammate.

320. Burns, *Baseball*.

321. "Dixie Walker"

322. "Ben Chapman"

323. Ibid.

BIBLIOGRAPHY

"5 Common Causes of PTSD in Law Enforcement." Outside the Badge. https://outsidethebadge.com.

"About Amadou." *The Amadou Diallo Foundation*. https://www.amadoudiallo.com/about-amadou/.

Adams, Cecil. "2, 4, 8, 16, ... how can you always have MORE ancestors as you go back in time?" *The Straight Dope*, August 21, 1987. https://web.archive.org.

"Amy Cooper (Central Park Karen)." *Vantu News*. https://www.vantunews.com.

Anando. "It's now a proven fact – Your unconscious mind is running your life!" *Life Trainings*. http://www.lifetrainings.com.

Associated Press "Penn State settlements covered 1971 Sandusky abuse claim." *USA Today*, May 8, 2016. http://www.usatoday.com.

Bargh, John, Mark Chen & Lara Burrows. "Automaticity of social behavior: Direct effects of trait construct and stereotype activation on action." *Journal of Personality and Social Psychology*, 71, 1996.

Bell, Susan. "Researcher uses DNA to demonstrate just how closely everyone on Earth is related to everyone else," August 8, 2013. https://phys.org/news/2013-08-dna-earth.html.

"Ben Chapman." https://en.wikipedia.org/wiki/Ben_Chapman_(baseball).

Bennett, Sid. *Seconds from Disaster, Columbia's Last Flight*, June 25, 2005. National Geographic.

Berman, Mark. "Prosecutors Say Dylann Roof 'Self-radicalized' Online, Wrote Another Manifesto in Jail." *The Washington Post*, August 22, 2016. https://www.washingtonpost.com.

"Bobby Bragan." https://en.wikipedia.org/wiki/Bobby_Bragan.

Bradberry, Travis and Greaves, Jean. *The Emotional Intelligence Quick Book.* New York: Fireside, 2005.

Bradley, Garrett. *Trial by Media, 3, 41 Shots.* May 11, 2020, https://www.netflix.com.

Brockmole, James. "Holding a Toy Gun Makes You Think Others Are Too, New Research Shows." *Notre Dame News,* March 19, 2012. https://news.nd.edu.

Burns, Ken. *Baseball, Episode 6, The National Pastime.* Florentine Films, Baseball Film Project, Inc., and WETA-TV, PBS, September 25, 1994.

"Calls for Justice After Elijah McClain's Death Resurfaces." American Autism Association, June 30, 2020. https://www.myautism.org.

"CBS News Investigates Police Reforms Including Implicit-Bias Training." CBS News, August 7, 2019. https://www.cbsnews.com.

Clifton, Jim. "The World's Broken Workplace." Gallup, June 13, 2017. https://news.gallup.com.

"Clyde Sukeforth." https://en.wikipedia.org/wiki/Clyde_Sukeforth.

Correll, Joshua, Bernadette Park, Charles M. Judd and Bernd Wittenbrink. "The Police Officer's Dilemma: Using Ethnicity to Disambiguate Potentially Threatening Individuals." *Journal of Personality and Social Psychology* 83, 6, 2002.

"Cracking the Code of Life." PBS, 2001. https://www.pbs.org/wgbh/nova/genome/.

Decker, Theodore, Joanne Viviano, Mike Wagner, Holly Zachariah. "Former Mount Carmel doctor William Husel has complicated past." *The Columbus Dispatch,* January 31, 2019. https://www.dispatch.com.

"Dixie Walker." https://en.wikipedia.org/wiki/Dixie_Walker.

Domonell, Kristen. "This Is Your Body On Fear." *UW Medicine,* October 25, 2017. https://rightasrain.uwmedicine.org.

Doyle, Jack. "Reese & Robbie, 1945-2005." *Pop History Dig,* June 29, 2011, updated February 1, 2019. https://www.pophistorydig.com.

Eberhardt, Jennifer, Phillip Atiba Goff, Valerie Purdie, & Paul Davies. "Seeing Black: Race, Crime, and Visual Processing." *Journal of Personality and Social Psychology* 87, 6, 2004.

Eberhardt, Jennifer. *Biased: Uncovering the Hidden Prejudice That Shapes What We See, Think, and Do.* New York, NY: Viking, 2019.

"Economic Impact of the Human Genome Project." Battelle (PDF).

Espalage, Dorothy Therese Pigott, & Joshua Polanin. "A Meta-Analysis of School-Based Bullying Prevention Programs' Effects on Bystander Intervention Behavior." *School Psychology Review* 41, 1, 2012.

Feldblum, Chai and Victoria Lipnic. EEOC Select Task Force on the Study of Harassment in the Workplace: report of co-chairs Chai R. Feldblum & Victoria A. Lipnic, 2016.

Fields, Douglas. "Humans Are Genetically Predisposed to Kill Each Other." *Psychology Today,* October 2, 2016. https://www.psychologytoday.com.

"Fight for Equality." GLAAD. https://www.glaad.org.

"Fight-or-Flight Reaction," *Changing Minds,* http://changingminds.org.

Ford, Dana. Juror: "'No Doubt' that George Zimmerman Feared for His Life," CNN, July 16, 2013, http://www.cnn.com.

Forero, Juan. "Serial Rapist Gets 155 Years; Judge Suggests His Crimes Contributed to Diallo Shooting." *The New York Times,* August 2, 2000. https://www.nytimes.com.

Fritsch, Jane. "The Diallo Verdict: The Overview; 4 Officers In Diallo Shooting Are Acquitted Of All Charges." *The New York Times,* February 26, 2000. https://www.nytimes.com.

Futty, John. "Attorney for Dr. Husel plans to build an uncomplicated defense." *The Columbus Dispatch,* January 31, 2020. https://www.dispatch.com.

Gandbhir, Geeta & Pollard, Sam. *Why We Hate, 3, Tools and Tactics,* October 27, 2019. https://www.netflix.com.

Gladwell, Malcolm. *Blink.* Little, Brown, and Co., New York, NY, 2005. Goleman, Daniel. *Emotional Intelligence.* New York: Bantam, 1998.

Goleman, Daniel. *Social Intelligence: The New Science of Human Relationships.* New York, NY, Bantam, 2006.

Goleman, Daniel. *Working with Emotional Intelligence.* New York: Bantam, 1998.

Goodtimes, Johnny. "Jackie Robinson and the Phillies." *Philly Sports History,* April 15, 2011. http://phillysportshistory.com.

Gordon, Gregory. "Atrocity Speech Law: Foundation, Fragmentation, Fruition." *Oxford University Press*, 2017.

Greenwald, Anthony, Debbie McGhee and Jordan Schwartz. "Measuring Individual Differences in Implicit Cognition: The Implicit Association Test." *Journal of Personality and Social Psychology* 74, 6, 1998.

"Happy Chandler." https://en.wikipedia.org/wiki/Happy_Chandler.

Harner, Andrew. "Jackie Robinson's Struggle as the First Black Player in MLB," April 1, 2020. https://howtheyplay.com.

Harris, Kamala. *Twitter Post.* February 24, 2017, 11:09 PM. https://twitter.com/KamalaHarris.

Hassan, Adeel. "Ohio Doctor Charged With Killing 25 Patients in Fentanyl Overdoses." *The New York Times,* June 5, 2019. https://www.nytimes.com.

Hate Map. Southern Poverty Law Center. https://www.splcenter.org/hate-map.

Hoffman, Kelly, Sophie Trawalter, Jordan Axt & Norman Oliver. "Racial bias in pain assessment and treatment recommendations, and false beliefs about biological differences between Blacks and Whites," April 4, 2016. https://www.pnas.org/content/113/16/4296

"Human Genome Project FAQ." National Human Genome Research Institute, updated February 24, 2020. https://www.genome.gov/human-genome-project/Completion-FAQ.

Ingman, Max, Henrik Kaessmann, Svante Pääba, Ulf Gyllensten, "Mitochondrial genome variation and the origin of modern humans," *Nature*, Vol. 408 (2000).

"Jackie Robinson." https://en.wikipedia.org/wiki/Jackie_Robinson.

"Jackie Robinson Breaks Baseball's Color Barrier, 1945." *Eye Witness to History,* 2005. http://eyewitnesstohistory.com/robinson.htm.

Krogstad, Jens Manuel. "67 years after Jackie Robinson broke the color barrier, Major League Baseball looks very different," April 16, 2014. https://www.pewresearch.org.

Kashatus, William. "W-B native took a stand against poor treatment of Jackie Robinson." *Citizen's Voice,* April 12, 2014, updated April 17, 2020. https://www.citizensvoice.com.

Kelly, Howard & Burrage, Walter. "Sims, James Marion." *American Medical Biographies.* Baltimore: The Norman, Remington Company, 1920.

Kinnard, Meg. "Feds: Church shooting suspect entrenched in his beliefs." *Telegram,* August 23, 2016. https://www.telegram.com.

Kiragu, Andrew W. "The Death of Elijah McClain-reflections on living with autism while Black." *Minnesota Spokesman Recorder,* July 15, 2020. https://spokesman-recorder.com.

Kulbarsh, Pamela. "2015 Police Suicide Statistics." https://www.officer.com, January 15, 2016.

Lampe, Claire. "What We Know About the Killing of Elijah McClain." *The Cut,* updated August 11, 2020.

LeDoux, Joseph. *The Emotional Brain.* New York: Simon and Schuster, 1996.

Lerner, Barron. "Scholars Argue Over Legacy of Surgeon Who Was Lionized, Then Vilified." *The New York Times,* October 28, 2003. https://www.nytimes.com.

Levinson, Justine "Forgotten Racial Equality: Implicit Bias, Decision making, and Misremembering," *Duke Law Journal* 57, 2, 2007.

Levitan, Clarisse. "Why 85% of People Hate their Jobs." *Staff Squared,* December 3, 2019. https://www.staffsquared.com.

Madhani, Aamer. "University of Missouri fires professor Melissa Click." *USA TODAY,* February 25, 2016. https://www.usatoday.com.

Marshall, Lisa. "Speeches: For the average person speaking at a normal pace, what is the average pace, what is the typical number of words they can say in a minute," March 10, 2011. https://www.quora.com/Speeches-For-the-average-person.

McGuire, Lauren. "Who would you shoot?" *The Society Pages,* July 15, 2013. https://thesocietypages.org/socimages.

Saul McLeod. "The Milgram Shock Experiment." *Simply Psychology,* February 5, 2017. https://www.simplypsychology.org/milgram.html.

Muehlenbein, Michael. "Human Evolutionary Biology." *Cambridge University Press,* 192-213; Stephanie Pappas. "Odd Cause of Humans' Dark Skin Proposed." *Live Science,* February 26, 2014. https://www.livescience.com.

Narzaryan, Andrew. "I'm just different': The family of Elijah McClain, a 23-year-old Black man killed by Colorado cops almost a year ago, is still waiting for justice," *Yahoo News,* June 27, 2020. https://news.yahoo.com.

NASA's "Goddard Space Flight Center Diversity Programs." DDP Handout.

NBC 4 Staff. "Columbus police identify 'person of interest' from protest, attorney calls post 'inaccurate and reckless." NBC News, May 31, 2020. https://www.nbc4i.com.

Nordon, Jeanette. *Understanding the Human Brain: Lecture 26: Brain Plasticity.* Chantilly, VA: The Teaching Company, 2007.

Ortiz, Erik.. "Elijah McClain was injected with ketamine while handcuffed. Some medical experts worry about its use during police calls. NBC News, July 1, 2020. https://www.nbcnews.com.

Ortiz, Erik. "Ohio doctor charged with 25 counts of murder, accused of prescribing excessive doses of painkillers." NBC News, June 5, 2019. https://www.nbcnews.com.

Parry, Wynne. "Age Confirmed for 'Eve' Mother of All Humans." *Live Science,* August 18, 2010. https://www.livescience.com.

Pasha, Riz. "57 Dr. Bruce Lipton Quotes on the Biology of Belief." *Succeed Feed,* January 30, 2020. https://succeedfeed.com/dr-bruce-lipton-quotes. "Pee Wee Reese." https://en.wikipedia.org/wiki/Pee_Wee_Reese.

Pettigrew, Thomas. "The ultimate attribution error: Extending Allport's cognitive analysis of prejudice." *Personality and Social Psychology Bulletin* 5, 4, 1979

Reiher, Andrea. "What Happened to Amadou Diallo's Killers?" *Heavy,* May 11, 2020. https://heavy.com.

Riddick, Iain. *Seconds from Disaster, episode 44, Space Shuttle Challenger,* aired January 31, 2007, National Geographic.

Rosenberg, Rebecca. "Manhattan DA charges Amy Cooper over viral Central Park 911 call. *New York Post.* https://nypost.com.

Roy, Beth. *41 Shots ... and Counting.* Syracuse, NY: Syracuse University Press, 2009.

Sapolsky, Robert. *Stress and Your Body: Stress, Learning and Memory.* Chantilly, VA: The Teaching Company, 2010.

Sapolsky, Robert. *Stress and Your Body: Stress and the Biology of Depression.* Chantilly, VA: The Teaching Company, 2010.

Showalter, Monica. "Turns out 'Central Park Karen' was an Obama and Buttigieg donor." *American Thinker,* May 27, 2020. https://www.americanthinker.com.

Siese, April. "White woman fired from her job after she called the cops on a black man in Central Park." *CBS News,* May 27, 2020. https://www.cbsnews.com.

Sommers, Samuel. "On Racial Diversity and Group Decision Making: Identifying Multiple Effects of Racial Composition on Jury Deliberations." *Journal of Personality and Social Psychology,* 90, 4, 2006.

Sommers, Samuel, & Phoebe Ellsworth. "Race in the Courtroom: Perceptions of Guilt and Dispositional Attributions." *Personality and Social Psychology Bulletin* 26, 11, 2000.

Samuel Sommers & Phoebe Ellsworth, "White Juror Bias: An Investigation of Prejudice Against Black Defendants in the American Courtroom." *Psychology, Public Policy, and Law* 7, 1, 2001.

Spatz, Lionel. "Dixie Walker." *Society for American Baseball Research.* https://sabr.org/bioproj/person/dixie-walker-2/#.

Spettel, Sarah & Mark Donald. "The Portrayal of J. Marion Sims' Controversial Surgical Legacy." *The Journal of Urology* 185, 6, June 2011.

Stringer, Grant & Quincy Snowdon. "Unlikely Suspect: Those who knew Elijah balk at Aurora police account of his death." *Sentinel Colorado,* October 27, 2019. https://whatiamunity.com/elijah-mcclain/.

"Study Finds Americans See Black Men as Larger And More Threatening Than White Men of The Same Size." *APA,* March 13, 2017. https://www.apa.org.

Taylor, Victoria. "Unhappy in America: Nearly 70% of U.S. employees miserable at work, study finds," *New York Daily News,* January 28, 2015. https://www.nydailynews.com.

Thompson, Frank. "Dr. Charles L. Thomas and Branch Rickey: Making Promises and Battling Racism." *All Things Wildly Considered.* July 2, 2017. https://allthingswildlyconsidered.blogspot.com.

Thompson, Ginger & Pierre-Pierre, Garry. "Portrait of Slain Immigrant: Big Dreams and a Big Heart." *New York Times,* February 12, 1999. https://www.nytimes.com.

Thomson, Jeremy. "Humans did come out of Africa, says DNA." *Nature,* December 7, 2000. https://www.nature.com.

Tompkins, Lucy. "Here's What You Need To Know About Elijah McClain's Death." *The New York Times,* August 16, 2020. https://www.nytimes.com.

Umh, Ruth. "How Diversity Heads Are Steering Their Companies Through The COVID-19 Crisis," *Forbes,* April 16, 2020. https://www.forbes.com.

"USA Gymnastics sex abuse scandal," https://en.wikipedia.org/wiki/USA_Gymnastics_sex_abuse_scandal.

United States Department of Labor. Workplace Violence, Occupational Safety and Health Administration.

Vera, Amir and Ly, Laura. "White woman who called police on a black man bird-watching in Central Park has been fired." *CNN,* revised May 26, 2020. https://www.cnn.com.

Villarosa, Linda. "Myths about physical racial differences were used to justify slavery — and are still believed by doctors today." *New York Times,* August 14, 2019.

Wilson, John, Kurt Hugnberg, & Nicholas Rule. "Racial Bias in Judgments of Physical Size and Formidability: From Size to Threat." *Journal of Personality and Social Psychology* 113, 1, March 13, 2017.

Wilson, Scott. "Elijah McClain's death reflects failures of White, suburban police departments," *Washington Post,* September 3, 2020. https://www.msn.com.

Wong, Sharon. "Making Space for Everyone: The Diversity Journal at NASA Goddard." Society for Human Resource Management's National Diversity Conference, Philadelphia, Pennsylvania, October 19, 2007.

Wyatt, Ronald. "Pain and Ethnicity." *AMA Journal of Ethics,* May 2013. https://journalofethics.ama-assn.org

ABOUT THE AUTHOR

Scott Warrick, JD, MLHR, CEQC, SHRM-SCP is both a practicing Employment Law Attorney and Human Resource Professional with almost 40 years of hands-on experience. Scott uses his unique background to help organizations get to where they want to go, which includes coaching and training managers and employees in his  own unique, practical, entertaining, and humorous style.

By training managers and employees on-site and virtually on over 50 topics that Scott customizes for his clients, he combines the areas of law and human resources to help organizations "solve employee problems before they start." Although he specializes in employment law, Scott's goal is *not* to win lawsuits, but rather to *prevent them* while improving employee morale.

His book, *Solve Employee Problems Before They Start: Resolving Conflict in the Real World,* is #1 for New Releases on Amazon for Conflict Resolution books, was named one of the best global Customer and Employee books for 2020-2021 by EGLOBALIS, and is also a Society for Human Resource Management best seller.

Scott's online *Do It Yourself HR Department,* his *Master HR Tool Kit Subscription,* and his book, *The HR Professional's Complete Guide to Federal Employment & Labor Law,* are favorites among HR professionals for helping them stay informed on regularly updated changes in law.

He is recognized as one of Business First's 20 People to Know In HR, CEO Magazine's 2008 Human Resources "Superstar," a Nationally Certified Emotional Intelligence Instructor, and a SHRM National Diversity Conference Presenter in 2003, 2006, 2007, 2008, and 2012.

He is also the recipient of the Human Resource Association of Central Ohio's Linda Kerns Award for Outstanding Creativity in the Field of HR Management and The Ohio State Human Resource Council's David Prize for Creativity in HR Management.

Scott's academic background and awards include Capital University College of Law (Class Valedictorian and Summa Cum Laude), Master of Labor & Human Resources, and a B.A. in Organizational Communication from The Ohio State University.

Scott can be reached at www.scottwarrick.com

Made in the USA
Monee, IL
15 October 2021